IRISH TEXTS S

THE FIRST HUNDRED YEARS

Cumann na Scribheann nGaedhilge
Subsidiary Series 9
1998

The Irish Texts Society: The First Hundred Years
Edited by Pádraig Ó Riain

First published by the Irish Texts Society
(Subsidiary Series No. 9) June 1998

ISBN 1 870166 88 4

Cover Illustration: Minutes of the Inaugural General Meeting of the Irish Texts Society held on 26 April 1898.

The Irish Texts Society
c/o Royal Bank of Scotland
Drummonds Branch
49 Charing Cross
Admiralty Arch
London SW 1A 2DX

Media Conversion and layout by
Diskon Technical Services Limited, Dublin 8.
Designed and printed by the
Elo Press Limited, Dublin 8.

Contents

Contributors

Neil Buttimer lectures in the Department of Modern Irish, University College, Cork.

D. Ellis Evans is Emeritus Professor of Celtic at Jesus College, Oxford. He has been a member of Council of the Irish Texts Society since 1978 and was President from 1983 to 1992.

Kevin Murray is a Toyota Scholar in the Department of Early and Medieval Irish, University College, Cork.

Brian Ó Cuív is retired Senior Professor at the Dublin Institute for Advanced Studies. He has been a member of Council of the Irish Texts Society since 1984.

Pádraig Ó Riain is Professor of Early and Medieval Irish, University College, Cork. He has been a member of Council of the Irish Texts Society since 1976 and President since 1992.

Pádraigín Riggs lectures in the Department of Modern Irish, University College, Cork.

Foreword

The editor has incurred many debts of gratitude in the preparation of this volume, especially to the other contributors for their unfailing co-operation but also to fellow members of Council for encouragement and assistance. The greatest of these latter debts was to the Honorary General Editor of the Society, Dr Brendan Bradshaw, who, despite illness, read and commented helpfully on several chapters. Dr Bradshaw also gave welcome advice concerning the lay-out of the volume. Valuable comments on the chapters relating to the archives of the Society were made by Council members M. J. Burns, D. Ellis Evans, M. Herbert, S. Hutton, B. Ó Buachalla, B. Ó Cuív and D. Sexton. The editor is also indebted to K. Murray for provision of the General Index and Bibliography.

Among many others who in one way or another facilitated the preparation of the volume were H. Davis and her staff in the Boole Library, University College, Cork; B. Doran, Librarian, Royal College of Surgeons, Dublin; Prof. J. Kelly, St John's College, Oxford; N. Kissane, National Library of Ireland; G. MacMahon, London; J. Maxwell, College Archives and S. Moore, Early Printed Books at Trinity College, Dublin; Prof. S. Ó Coileáin, Department of Modern Irish, University College, Cork; Dr R. Refaussé, Church of Ireland Library, Dublin and E. Uí Cheallacháin, former Secretary, Combined Departments of Irish, University College, Cork.

Agus an chéad imleabhar den phríomhshraith á sheoladh aige in 1899, luaigh Cathaoirleach an Chumainn, F. York Powell, rannta as dán le hAodh Buí Mac Cruitín. B'í éirim na rannta gur scrios ollmhór é dá dtráfaí 'tiobraid an fhis' is dá gceilfí 'leabhair uama a's iris'. Tar éis dó caoga naoi 'leabhair uama a's iris' a fhoilsiú ina phríomhshraith agus naoi gcinn eile ina shraith thánaisteach, ní misde do Chumann na Scríbheann nGaedhilge a mhaíomh go bhfuil a chion déanta aige le céad blian anuas chun a dheimhniú ná tráfaí an tobar feasa úd. Nára lú an rath ar shaothar an Chumainn sna blianta atá roimhe.

Pádraig Ó Riain,
Uachtarán, Cumann na Scríbheann nGaedhilge,
Meitheamh 1998.

Assessments

Chapter One

The Beginnings of the Society

Pádraigín Riggs

Douglas Hyde's *The Story of Early Gaelic Literature*[1] was reviewed in *The Manchester Guardian* of 9 April 1895 by Frederick York Powell. In the course of his review York Powell asked: 'Is it too much to hope for the establishment of an Irish Text (sic) Society?' This was probably the first ever reference to an 'Irish Text Society' and, in the words of Oliver Elton, 'the wish... [was] prophetic'.[2] Three years later York Powell chaired the Inaugural General Meeting of the Irish Texts Society and when, on this occasion, he spoke of the necessity that had existed for the establishment of such a society,[3] he was merely restating the case he had made in his 1895 review. There he had urged that it 'should publish in handy, clear-printed form the unpublished texts of each division of the tongue, early, old, middle, and modern Irish, with versions, if possible, into plain English or Latin, as may be most convenient', and had accurately foreseen that there was 'matter enough unprinted to keep such a society going for a century'.[4] York

1 Published in London (1895) for the 'New Irish Library'.

2 O. Elton, *Frederick York Powell, Vol. I: Memoirs and Letters* (Oxford, 1906) 183. In the report on the Inaugural Meeting of the Society which appeared in *Fáinne an Lae* (7 May, 1898) the initial suggestion that an Irish Texts Society be established is attributed to Frederick York Powell:

> It speaks well for the reviving interest in Gaelic Studies that the Irish Texts Society was able, within four months of the issue of their prospectus, to announce their inaugural meeting for Tuesday last. Professor York Powell, *to whose suggestion the idea of the Society owes its origin*, occupied the chair ...

3 See the First Annual Report of the Irish Texts Society, published as an appendix to D. Hyde, ed., *Giolla an Fhiugha* (London, 1899) v-vii.

4 The review continued:

> It is a disgrace to Irishmen that they have neglected their own tongue, and contented themselves with the thin culture to be drawn from rhetorical English speeches of Irishmen from the end of the last and the early years of this century, and with a few verse translations that smother half the beauties of the original. It is the alien and the immigrant in Erin that have done most of the work that has rendered most of the oldest MSS. available to us. It is a Frenchman who is making the Irish laws accessible to the student of ancient

Powell was aware of the work being done at the time by scholars in other languages to make literature from an earlier period accessible to contemporary readers. Appointed Regius Professor of Modern History at Oxford in 1894, he was known primarily for his work on Scandinavian literature but was also an authority on Old English and Old French, and in proposing the establishment of an Irish Texts Society he almost certainly had in mind such models as the Early English Text Society which had been established in 1864 and La Société des Anciens Textes Français which had been established in 1875.[5]

However, although York Powell may have been the first person to use the term 'Irish Text Society', he was not the first to perceive the need for such an organisation.[6] Bodies such as the Irish Archaeological Society (founded in 1840), the Celtic Society (founded in 1845) – two bodies united from 1862 as the Irish Archaeological and Celtic Society – and the Ossianic Society (founded in 1853) had

institutions, and an Englishman who has secured the printing of unpublished texts and traditions, which Irish publishers will not attempt. It is no use disputing where the fault lies for all this, if it is not being bettered (*Manchester Guardian*, 9 April, 1895).

5 In fact, in his Preface to *Giolla an Fhiugha*, York Powell, writing as chairman of the Irish Texts Society, referred specifically to the example of both of these societies, as well as to the example of the Scandinavian Texts Societies, the Ossianic Society and the Irish Archaeological Society.

6 It is interesting to note here what Georges Dottin had to say at about this time in his review of Hyde's *The Story of Early Gaelic Literature*, which appeared in *Annales de Bretagne*, vol. X, No. 3 (April, 1895):

> L'époque la plus brillante de cette littérature est sans contredit le moyen-age, mais tous les efforts des celtistes semblent avoir eu pour but de ne faire connaitre que les plus anciens monuments épiques de l'Irlande. On s'est peu occupé des poèmes ossianiques qui, sous la forme que leur avait donnée Macpherson, ont eu au commencement de ce siècle un si grand succès. On ignore à peu près complètement les noms des poètes de l'époque danoise (Xe-XIe siècles). M. Douglas Hyde nous donne sur ces deux périodes d'intéressants renseignements. Il faut espérer que la méthode qui consistait à commencer l'étude de l'irlandais par l'irlandais ancien, lequel présente de grandes difficultés et ne peut s'éclairer que par l'irlandais moderne, sera peu à peu abandonnée, et qu'on partira enfin du connu pour arriver à la connaissance de l'inconnu. Il serait à désirer que les Irlandais en possession de la langue moderne se missent à l'étude de l'irlandais moyen et de l'irlandais ancien. Puisse le livre de M. Hyde susciter en Irlande de nombreux travailleurs! Les continentaux ne feront que se réjouir de la concurrence scientifique qui leur sera faite.

all been engaged in the editing and publication of texts in the Irish language. In 1880 the philologist Ernst Windisch issued the first volume of his *Irische Texte* in Leipzig, and when the Gaelic Union came into existence in that same year, it also engaged in publishing texts. In 1889, however, the nature of the material being published by these organisations became the subject of a debate in the correspondence columns of *The Academy.* Over a period of several months letters appeared in that review from a number of scholars including Whitley Stokes, John Rhys, Standish H. O'Grady, John Fleming and Kuno Meyer under the heading 'Old Irish and the Spoken Language'[7].

The debate was initiated by the philologist, Whitley Stokes, who made disparaging references to modern Irish and these references elicited a response from John Fleming of the Gaelic Union who was at the time editor of *The Gaelic Journal.* Fleming criticised Stokes and certain non-native philologists for their lack of knowledge of the spoken language. The native scholars were, in turn, reproached for their failure to publish material in the modern tongue. In a letter to the review dated 5 October 1889 Alfred Nutt, the London publisher, who was also known as a folklorist and celticist, was of the view that 'well-directed energy and proper organisation would enable a series of Irish classics of the last four or five centuries to be brought out without loss to the promoters'.[8] The subsequent issue of *The Academy*, dated 12 October 1889, contained a reply from Thomas Flannery. A native of County Mayo, Flannery had lived in England from the age of seven.[9] His family spoke Irish, but it was at school in Manchester that he learned to read and write the Irish language. Having trained as a teacher at the Catholic Training College at Hammersmith, he subsequently taught English and Latin at several Training Colleges in Manchester and London – including his own alma mater, Hammersmith. At the same time he wrote extensively on the Irish

7 See the discussion of this correspondence, particularly with reference to the philological movement, in S. Ó Lúing, *Kuno Meyer 1858-1919* (Dublin, 1991) 25 - 27.

8 Nutt added: 'At present the great body of Irishmen have only themselves to blame if their interest in their native tongue is held to be purely Platonic'. In this instance, again, it could be claimed that 'the wish was prophetic'!

9 See D. Ó Liatháin, *Tomas Ó Flannghaile, Scoláire agus File* (Dublin, no date).

language and Irish literature[10] and also lectured on the subject. In his letter Flannery took Nutt to task for the latter's attack on Irish publishers, pointing out the achievements of the Gaelic Union in making texts in the living language available. Nevertheless he concluded his letter with the plea that publishers should show less interest in 'ancient and medieval tracts' and 'give us something of modern times, with some kind of human interest in it, ...cheap grammars, cheap dictionaries, history, biography, legends, stories, poems, sketches, books of religion and devotion'.

At the time Flannery wrote, the popular language revival organisation which would be the Gaelic League had not yet been founded. That organisation would in time provide at least some of the material Flannery sought. However, when the initiative to establish what was to be known as the Irish Texts Society eventually came in 1896, it did not come from the Gaelic League[11] – nor, indeed, from any organisation based in Ireland. It came from the London based Irish Literary Society which appointed a provisional sub-committee early in that year to consider the feasibility of such an enterprise.[12] Thomas Flannery played an important part in the work of that body.

---

10 The first edition of Flannery's book, *For the Tongue of the Gael*, was published in 1896 and contained a dozen articles and reviews which had first appeared, as the author himself says in the Preface, 'in various Dublin and London periodicals' over the previous fourteen years. The second edition, published in 1907, contained four additional essays.

11 This statement is not intended as a criticism of the very important work being carried out by the Gaelic League at that time. In fact, as the following extract from that organisation's weekly paper, *Fáinne an Lae*, for the week after the Inaugural Meeting of the Texts Society demonstrates, a close connection existed between the two bodies:

> In connection with the Irish Texts Society it is noteworthy that not only is its President, Dr Douglas Hyde, President of the Gaelic League, but all its Executive Council, with the exception of Professor Yorke (sic) Powell and Mr. Alfred Nutt, are prominent members of the same body. (7 May 1898, p. 8.)

12 See the First Annual Report of the Irish Texts Society. In fact, the project was mentioned in the Literary Society's annual report for 1895-6:

> The new work under consideration by the general committee comprises the following schemes: the formation of an Irish Text Society ... The Irish Text Society will undertake the translation and publication of the more modern Irish works which the antiquarian or archaeological bodies have hitherto neglected or ignored. Many offers of support have already been received. (*The Academy*, 14 March 1896, p. 220.)

Any study of the origin of the Texts Society necessarily commences with the Irish Literary Society which was founded in 1892[13] and had as its objectives: (1) to afford a centre of social and literary intercourse for persons of Irish nationality and (2) to promote the study of the Irish language, Irish history, literature, music and art. An organisation of this kind was not unusual in the London of the late nineteenth century. In its aims, the Irish Literary Society resembled the Viking Club[14] and The Honourable Society of the Cymmrodorion,[15] to mention just two examples. There were many similarities also between it and an earlier Irish Literary Society.

Despite the overlap of personnel and the similarity of objectives, the ILS and its predecessor of the same name (formerly the Southwark Literary Club) were separate organisations. According to its founder, Frank Fahy, a civil servant from Kinvarra, Co. Galway, it was the 'need for self-education' which led to the establishment of the Southwark Irish Literary Club in 1883. The aims of this club were: 'to cultivate and spread among adults a knowledge of Irish history, language, art and literature and to serve as a medium of social and intellectual intercourse for Irish people of both sexes'.[16] The lecturers who addressed its modest gatherings included T. F. Flannery, R. Barry

13 For a contemporary account of the foundation of the Irish Literary Society, see W. P. Ryan, *The Irish Literary Revival* (London, 1894) chapter IV. See also G. MacMahon, *The Origins of the Irish Literary Society, London, with some notes on the early years*, (a paper read to the Society on 1 June 1993) and *Souvenir Programme of the Coming of Age of the Irish Literary Society of London* (1892-1913). Certain aspects of the early history of the Society are also dealt with by R. F. Foster in *W. B. Yeats: A Life* (Oxford, 1997) Chapter 5.

14 The Viking Club originated in 1892 as a 'Social and Literary Branch' of the Orkney and Shetland (Charitable) Society of London. In 1893, having formally adopted the title 'Viking Club' or 'Orkney, Shetland and Northern Society', along with a new constitution, this organisation extended its membership 'to all interested in Northern studies'. See *Saga-Book of the Viking Club* (London) Vol. I, part 1, (reprinted in 1980 by A. M. S. Press, New York, for the Viking Society for Northern Research).

15 This society, originally founded in 1751 and revived in 1873, described its especial aims as 'the improvement of education and the promotion of intellectual culture by the encouragement of Literature, Science and Arts, as connected with Wales'.

16 The source of this quotation and of the subsequent information regarding the Southwark Literary Club is the unpublished text of a talk given by Frank Fahy to the Irish Literary Society in 1921, entitled 'Ireland in London - Reminiscences'. A copy of this speech was kindly lent to me by Mr. Gerald MacMahon of London.

O'Brien, W. B. Yeats, Sophie Bryant and Edmond Downey. When the Club moved from Southwark to Clapham early in 1890 it was decided to change its name to the Irish Literary Society. Following its relocation, however, the activities of the society went into decline. When a new organisation was formed in 1892,[17] it assumed the name of what was by then the defunct Irish Literary Society and it included a significant proportion of the latter's former membership.[18]

Following the pattern established by the Southwark Club, and in accordance with its own stated aims, the Literary Society organised regular lectures on topics related to Ireland. Flannery was the chosen lecturer on several of these occasions.[19] Others included Laurence Ginnell, T. W. Rolleston and R. Barry O'Brien. The Inaugural Address for the session 1894-95 was delivered by the President of the newly formed Gaelic League, Dr Douglas Hyde, who came from Ireland to speak on 'The Last Three Centuries of Gaelic Literature'. According to Dr Mark Ryan, a branch of the Gaelic League was formed in the Society as a direct result of this lecture,[20] (though this 'branch' may simply have consisted of Irish language classes).[21]

As well as organising lectures, the new society also had plans to issue a series of books which would be known as the 'Library of Ireland'. These plans soon became a source of conflict between Yeats

---

17 This organisation had its origin in a meeting held in December 1891 in the Chiswick home of W. B. Yeats.

18 As Frank Fahy pointed out in his talk to the Literary Society in 1921:

> From this meeting sprang, 29 years ago, the present Irish Literary Society, in the roll of Original Members of which I find the names of 17 of my Southwark friends, seven of whom were on its first Committee …

19 He is described in the *Gaelic Journal* of December 1894, as 'Mr. Thomas O'Flannaoile, Celtic scholar and lecturer in Irish to the London Irish Literary Society'. The February 1995 issue of the same paper informs us that 'Mr. Thomas O'Flannaoile delivered, on January 9, a lecture on the Irish language, under the auspices of the Irish Literary Society, at the Medical Hall, Thames Embankment, London'.

20 *Fenian Memories* (Dublin, 1946) 162.

21 This 'branch' may in fact have consisted of the Irish classes taught by Thomas Flannery which were organised under the auspices of The Irish Literary Society and to which Eleanor Hull refers in the 1913 *Souvenir Programme*. See Ó Liatháin, *Tomás Ó Flannghaile*, 23. Indeed, this probably explains the reference in *The Gaelic Journal* of March 1895, to 'Connradh na Gaeilge, Londain', as the London Gaelic League was not established until October 1896. (See *The Gaelic Journal*, November 1896, 112).

and the President of the society, Sir Charles Gavan Duffy, who each had a different idea of what the 'Library of Ireland' should be producing.[22] When the project was eventually launched, the editor of what was now to be known as 'The New Irish Library' was Sir Charles Gavan Duffy, with Dr Douglas Hyde as assistant-editor for the National Literary Society in Dublin, and T. W. Rolleston (and subsequently R. Barry O'Brien) as assistant-editor for the Irish Literary Society. It was as part of this series that Hyde's *The Story of Early Gaelic Literature* was published in 1895.

The plea made by Frederick York Powell in his *Manchester Guardian* review for the establishment of an Irish Texts Society was echoed two months later, on 8 June 1895, at a joint meeting of the Irish Literary Society and the Viking Club.[23] The lecturer on this occasion was Dr George Sigerson who spoke on 'Kelts and Sea-Kings', and the chairman who introduced him was Karl Blind, a leading member of the Viking Club. Blind, a German-born political refugee who had settled in London, had a particular interest in heroic literature,[24] and in the course of his introductory speech he emphasised the need for 'such charming Irish poems and romances as "The Lay of Oisín or the Land of the Young", "The Children of Lir", "The Pursuit of Diarmaid and Gráinne" or "The Youthful Exploits of Fionn"' to be made accessible in 'sufficiently attractive English translations'. He felt that 'something might be done in this respect similar to what Simrock did in German for the Edda, for Beowulf and for the Medieval heroic and other poetry of his country'.[25] Amongst those present at this meeting[26] were: Dr Mark Ryan, Alfred Percival Graves, G. A. Greene, Laurence

---

22 For a contemporary account of this controversy, see Ryan, *The Irish Literary Revival,* Chapter IV. See also Foster, *W. B. Yeats*, Chapter V.

23 Apparently such joint meetings were not unusual. For example 'a joint meeting of the Gaelic Society of London, the Irish Literary Society and the Irish Gaelic League' was held on 12 February 1898, when a paper was read on the subject of 'The Norsemen in Scotland'. (See the 'Proceedings of the Viking Club' in *Saga-Book*, vol. II, p. 132.) While Frederick York Powell's name is not one of those mentioned as having attended the meeting of 8 June 1895, this does not mean he was not present. We know that he was a member of the Viking Club, and that he delivered that society's Inaugural Address for 1894.

24 A report of this meeting in the *Daily News* of 11 June refers to Blind's interest in the *Oceanic* (sic) Saga. Perhaps the title of Dr Sigerson's lecture suggested the homonym!

25 See *Saga-Book*, Vol. I, pp. 151-2.

26 See *The Freeman's Journal*, 10 June 1895.

Ginnell B.L., W. B. Yeats (the poet was then so little known that his name was written 'Teats'), Michael McDonagh and F. A. Fahy. Eleanor Hull is mentioned as having taken part in the discussion which followed the lecture.

It is not possible to say to what extent the decision to establish an Irish Texts Society was triggered by this discussion. However, the fact that the initiative should have come at this time from a London-based rather than an Irish organisation is undoubtedly due to the opportunity which the Irish Literary Society afforded for interaction between those individuals who were also members of other societies like the Viking Club, the Folklore Society and the Early English Text Society, on the one hand, and those who were active in the Irish Revival Movement, on the other hand. The important role played by the publication of Hyde's *Story of Early Gaelic Literature* in drawing attention to the dearth of published texts should not be underestimated either.[27]

It was announced in the Annual Report of the Irish Literary Society for the year 1895-6 that 'preliminary steps have been taken to form an Irish Text (sic) Society for the publication of modern Irish works' through the establishment of a sub-committee for the purpose. This included 'Mr. Flannery (Chairman), Dr Norman Moore, Messrs. Goddard Orpen, G. A. Greene, F. A. Fahy, J. G. O'Keeffe, D. Mescal, D. Comyn, Dr Hyde, Dr Joyce and Dr Sigerson'.[28] One of the first tasks undertaken by this sub-committee was the preparation of a circular outlining the objectives of the proposed society with a view to obtaining support from interested persons. Most of this preliminary work seems to have been carried out by Thomas Flannery. In a letter to David Comyn, dated 22 April 1896, Flannery wrote: 'We intend issuing a circular on behalf of the projected Irish Texts Society and we think it advisable to mention in it a few of the works which have not

27 The importance of Douglas Hyde's role in the Society is further enhanced by the fact that not only would he be its first President but also by the fact that the Society's first published volume would be edited by him.

28 *The Gaelic Journal*, May 1896. According to the Minutes of the Irish Texts Society, the Original 'Provisional Committee' of 1896 consisted of: D. Comyn, Dr A. Colles, F. A. Fahy, T. J. Flannery, G. A. Greene, D. Hyde, P. W. Joyce, J. McNeill, J. G. O'Keeffe, Goddard Orpen, G. Sigerson. The following names were added by the General Committee in May 1897: R. Barry O'Brien, R. Stewart Macalister, Norma Borthwick, Eleanor Hull, M. O'Sullivan. See also note 11 above and p. 104 below.

yet been published and which it is desirable to have'.[29] A subsequent letter made it clear, however, that the Sub-Committee's initial efforts were encountering difficulties so that it became necessary 'to postpone action in the matter of the proposed Irish Texts Society'.[30] In spite of Flannery's pessimism, some progress seems to have been achieved by the beginning of the autumn session. A version of the proposed circular referred to in the letter of 22 April had materialised and had been sent to the press.[31] However, the actual circular (or the

---

29 Flannery went on to state:

> I have never seen O'Mahony's Keating - is the Irish text published in it – and in full? If it is of course we shan't want it again. Write down in the enclosed slip the names of three or four works known to yourself which have never yet been published and return to me at once, please. There are many things, I believe, in the British Museum and at Oxford but you might keep to what there is in Dublin or elsewhere in Ireland. This is a branch of the subject I am not so familiar with as I ought to be (MS. 8467 (Comyn), Folder 24, National Library of Ireland).

30 The postponement was until October. Flannery's letter continued:

> I don't know if anything will come of it or whether any such society will result. Very few of our members take any interest in the matter. The strong unionist element is not only indifferent but really hostile - their only idea of "Irish" literature is books in English, published in London. Above all things the *national* idea (both at home and abroad) is weak now, bleaker than it has ever been for years - and the prevalence of this idea has - I hold - always been the root and source of all efforts on behalf of our native literature. (Ibid. Letter from Flannery to Comyn dated 24 August 1896).

31 The following report which appeared in *The Speaker* on 21 November was clearly based on such a document:

> The Irish Literary Society which has already done such excellent work for the Celtic literature of Ireland is about to open up a new sphere of useful activity for Irish scholars. It desires to print and edit Irish texts - not so much ancient and medieval texts, for which a good deal has been done already - but for the Irish texts of the last three or four centuries. There are enough of these to keep a society at work for several years to come, and it is therefore proposed to form an Irish Texts Society with an annual subscription of 10s 6d. The inclusion on the Provisional Committee of such well-known Irish scholars as Dr Sigerson, Mr. Flannery, Dr Hyde and Dr P. W. Joyce is a sufficient guarantee of competence. For the benefit of the comparative sociologist, or the merely bellettristic person, the texts will be accompanied by translations, and texts in other languages may also be published, if they throw new light on Irish history or life. One text and its translation, it is hoped, will be published each year. The address of the committee is 8, Adelphi Terrace, W. C. The scheme should attract all persons who are interested in that literature which until recent years has been so neglected by Irish Nationalists - unlike the Nationalists in every other country in Europe. It is true that Irish Nationalists have had to think of more pressing needs.

version of it which existed at this time) does not appear to have been generally distributed yet.[32] By December, Flannery was once again discouraged by the lack of response to the project and now expressed reservations about the membership of the Sub-Committee. Although the Irish Literary Society was based in London, the members of the Texts Society Sub-Committee included persons resident in both London and Dublin. In another letter to Comyn, having named some prominent accessions to the Society, such as 'Fr Hickey of Maynooth, Canon O'Hanlon of Dublin, Fr O'Laverty MRIA of Belfast', Flannery went on to say that 'the present provisional committee – at least the members living in London – feel that they should give way to a *permanent committee* composed mostly of men living in Ireland, for it is in Ireland you have most of the texts and most of the men to translate them'.[33] While it is true that most of the scholars who subsequently edited volumes for the Society were based in Ireland (and not all were men!), the permanent committee was – and continues to be – based in London with some of its members living in Ireland.

Flannery's dejection in the latter part of 1896 seems to have been justified as it appeared the project was in danger of being abandoned at that time. It is remarkable that in February 1897 Dr Arthur Conan Doyle,[34] in proposing the toast of the Irish Literary Society at that

---

This report reads like a paraphrase of certain sections of the printed circular, fourteen copies of which are to be found in the papers of Eoin MacNeill, Ms. 10,881 (Folder 18), National Library of Ireland. This circular is headed 'Proposed Irish Texts Society' and the address on it is that of the Irish Literary Society. The document is not dated though '1896' - the last digit crossed out, and followed by 7 – has been added in pencil. The full text of this circular can be found in Chapter 8 (1) below.

32 According to Eleanor Hull, the first circular was sent out in 1897. Writing in *The Irish Literary Society Gazette* (No. 3, Vol. I) in March 1899 she pointed out that:

> ... perhaps they [i. e. the Literary Society] never undertook a task of more urgent national importance than when they sent out their first circular in 1897 to feel its way towards the formation of an Irish Texts Society.

The minutes of the Texts Society Sub-Committee for 24 May, 1897 state that:

> Mr Flannery then made a statement with regard to the present position of the Texts Society; he said that *copies of the first circular* had been sent to all members of the ILS and a few to persons outside the Society both at home and abroad. Out of these about 50 promises of support had been obtained.

33 Flannery added, somewhat sadly: 'Some of these accessions I have no doubt are due to your exertions'. Ibid., dated 14 December, 1896.

34 The creator of Sherlock Holmes! He became *Sir* Arthur Conan Doyle in 1902, when he was knighted for his services as a medical doctor in the South African War.

society's annual dinner, spoke of the necessity for the editing and publication of the great body of Irish literature still only available in manuscripts, but did not mention the existence of the Texts Society Sub-Committee.[35] However, the May edition of *The Gaelic Journal* stated that it was 'glad to observe from the Annual Report of the Irish Literary Society, London, that its Irish classes are still continued and that the project of the Irish Texts Society has not been abandoned.[36] This report appears to have given a new impetus to the Texts Society project, with the result that what was heretofore designated as the 'Provisional' Sub-Committee now became the (Official) Sub-Committee, the first meeting of which took place on 24 May 1897. In fact, although the Provisional Sub-Committee had been active since the early months of 1896, the first recorded minutes we have are of that meeting. The attendance on 24 May 1897 included T. J. Flannery, Goddard Orpen, G. A. Greene, Dr A. Colles, R. Barry O'Brien, R. Stewart Macalister, J. G. O'Keeffe, Norma Borthwick and Eleanor Hull.

---

35 Conan Doyle said:

> A capable judge has told me that if all the unexamined Gaelic manuscripts, which are scattered from Dublin to the Vatican, were edited and published, there would be enough to make a thousand stout volumes. They deal with history, with sport, with folk-lore, with travels, with every conceivable subject. This is the huge quarry which is waiting for workers, and it is little to the credit either of Irish or of English scholarship that it is in Germany that the most work has hitherto been done. *Here, then, is a task for members of the Irish Literary Society* [my italics]. With a little money and a great deal of scholarship, how much might be done in that vast storehouse of materials, one little snippet of which, under the name of the Ossianic ballads, furnished the favourite reading of the greatest man whom this century has produced! (*The Gaelic Journal*, March 1897, p. 176. The report refers to a speech made on February 13th).

36 The paper then quotes from the Annual Report:

> Considerable support has been promised towards the contemplated Irish Texts Society – the intending subscribers including amongst them leading scholars and *savants* in Ireland, England, Scotland, France and the United States. A much greater number of subscribers, however, must be obtained before a publisher can be induced to undertake the bringing out of Irish Texts. It is believed that as soon as the project becomes widely known, the Committee will be put in a position to announce the permanent formation of the society and the early publication of an important Irish Text.

In total, the combined membership of both the Provisional Sub-Committee of 1896-7 and of the Sub-Committee of May 1897 numbered eighteen persons. Five of these – David Comyn, Douglas Hyde, Eoin Mac Neill, P. W. Joyce and George Sigerson – were resident in Ireland and were leading figures in the Irish Revival Movement. Of the remaining thirteen, five had been associated with the Southwark Literary Club: Frank Fahy, J. G. O'Keeffe, Thomas Flannery, Norma Borthwick (who learned Irish at the Club from Flannery) and R. Barry O'Brien.

The socio-economic and educational profile of the founder members is worthy of note here. Of the eighteen, four were civil servants: Fahy, Mescal, O'Sullivan and O'Keeffe. These four individuals represented a new type of Irish immigrant who began to arrive in the big cities of Britain, and particularly in London, in the last quarter of the nineteenth century. These young immigrants were educationally qualified for employment as clerks in the great Victorian cities, and in particular, since the introduction of competitive entrance examinations in 1870, for posts in the civil service. Some of these people came from an Irish-speaking background. Most were highly intelligent but without employment prospects at home and, while a clerkship in a London office offered them security, the work was neither stimulating nor demanding. It was mainly from this element of the Irish community in London that the various Irish organisations – especially the Gaelic League – drew their leading personnel.

Relatively little has been written about this important class of Irish immigrant, with the notable exception of an article by the late Martin J. Waters entitled 'Peasants and Emigrants: Considerations of the Gaelic League as a Social Movement'.[37] Waters based his analysis on a series called 'Pioneers' which consisted of some fifty-two sketches of individuals who had been involved in the Gaelic Revival. These sketches by W. P. Ryan were published in 1906 in *The Irish Peasant* of which Ryan was editor. The main weakness in Waters' analysis is the smallness of his representative sample; however, a fuller study of the kind he attempted is now possible, using the abundant data available in the five-volume *1882-1982: Beathaisnéis* series.[38]

37 D. J. Casey & R. E. Rhodes, eds., *Views of the Irish Peasantry, 1800 - 1900* (Connecticut, 1977) 160 - 174.

38 Edited by Diarmuid Breathnach and Máire Ní Mhurchú (Dublin, 1986 - 97).

It is interesting to note that the four founder members of the Irish Texts Society mentioned above all achieved senior posts in the civil service, in spite of Frank Fahy's comment on the uninspiring state of his own promotional prospects in his 1921 talk to the Literary Society.[39] One of the four, J. G. O'Keeffe, was awarded a C. B. E. for his service in the War Office during World War I.[40] Three of the eighteen other members were medical doctors (Sigerson, Colles and Moore).[41] Barry O'Brien was a lawyer.[42] Goddard Orpen was also a lawyer though he was better known as an antiquarian. G. A. Greene M. A. was an Examiner to the Board of Education and was one of the organisers of the Rhymers Club.[43] Described as 'the Pindar of

---

39 Fahy stated:

> I came to London in 1873 to take up a small appointment in the civil service … A six-hour day, 11 to 5, light, mechanical, uncongenial work; my superiors youngish men whose shoes would surely not grow cold for years; promotion barred from class to class - ambition slept, and one sank readily into routine and *laisser-faire*. A friend of mine who prided himself on the pulling of official wires once called on me at the office and asked me what were my prospects there. My desk was pleasantly placed near a 4th floor window with a fine outlook on the Thames. I took him to the window, and showing him the view from the Crystal Palace to London Bridge and across to the Surrey Hills, said: 'That's the only prospect I have here'. (See note 16 above.)

40 See Breathnach, Ní Mhurchú, *1882-1982: Beathaisnéis a Trí,* 113-114.

41 George Sigerson is described in ibid. *a hAon,* 112-3 as: translator, historian, archaeologist, medical doctor, neurologist, poet, zoologist, botanist, politician, journalist and Gaelic scholar! According to the entry under his name in ibid. *a Dó,* 70, Norman Moore was knighted in 1919 for his work on the history of St. Bartholomew's Hospital, London, where he worked as a medical doctor for most of his professional life. Though neither born in Ireland nor of Irish parents, he was a member of the council of the Society for the Preservation of the Irish Language and of the Gaelic Union. Dr Abraham Colles FRCSI (1874) was the grandson of the famous Dublin surgeon of the same name; see John F. Fleetwood, *History of Medicine in Ireland* (Dublin, 1951) 152-3.

42 In his portrait of Barry O'Brien in *The Irish Peasant* (21 July, 1906), W. P. Ryan says:

> He loves all Irish-Irelanders with the possible exception of Mr. D. P. Moran … He is a member of the Irish and English Bars, but is better known perhaps as a legal-minded literary man than as a literary-minded lawyer.

43 This group which was formed in London in 1890 included Edward Garnett, Lionel Johnson, John Todhunter and W. B. Yeats. Frederick York Powell was also associated with the group. See Norman Alford, *The Rhymers' Club: Poets of the Tragic Generation* (London, 1994).

Wakefield',[44] he translated the work of the Italian poet Giosue Carducci and published it in 1893 as *Italian Lyricists of Today.*[45] R. A. Stewart Macalister was an archaeologist, Eleanor Hull had learned Irish from Standish Hayes O'Grady and had studied under Kuno Meyer, Holger Pedersen and Robin Flower. As well as being a prominent member of the Irish Literary Society, she had an interest in Scandinavian culture, particularly in Icelandic, was secretary of the Royal Asian Society and was a member of the council of the Folklore Society. Norma Borthwick, having learned Irish from Thomas Flannery, like him, taught the language and wrote extensively on it.

When the The Irish Texts Society Sub-Committee met on 24 May 1897, T. J. Flannery was re-elected as Chairman. He had already been appointed Chairman of the Provisonal Sub-Committee one year previously. Norma Borthwick and Eleanor Hull were appointed to act as secretaries and R. A. Stewart Macalister became honorary treasurer. The main tasks undertaken by the body over the following eleven month period could be summarised under the following headings: finance, membership, the identification of suitable texts for editing, the appointment of editors and the procurement of a publisher. In the latter part of the year a good deal of attention was paid to the constitution of the society, that is, to the proposed membership of its various councils and committees. One of the very first issues addressed by the Sub-Committee was the nomination of a publisher. The names of three Dublin-based and four London-based publishers were proposed:

44 John Davidson, in a letter to William Symington McCormick (November 1891), quoted in John Sloan, ed., *Selected Poems and Prose of John Davidson* (Oxford, 1995) 175-7.

45 See Ryan, *The Irish Literary Revival*, 119. Born and educated in Florence, George Arthur Greene graduated from Trinity College, Dublin (B. A. 1876, M. A. 1879). He was the author of a collection of original poetry, *Songs of the Open Air* (London, 1912), and contributed poems to the *Book of the Rhymers' Club* (London, 1892) and *The Second Book of the Rhymers' Club* (London, 1894). In addition, he edited *The Life of Nelson* ('with introducton, notes and questions for examination', London, 1882) and *The Civil Wars in Peru* ('being an excerpt from Presscott's History of the Conquest of Peru', London, 1880). As well as translating Carducci from Italian, Greene translated two works from German, *The Architecture of Classical Antiquity and of the Renaissance* by Josef Bühlmann (Berlin, 1892) and (in collaboration with A. C. Hillier and his fellow Rhymer, Ernest Dowson) Volume 1 of Richard Muther's *History of Modern Painting* (London, 1895). For an obituary and letter concerning Greene, see *The Irish Book Lover* 13 (Aug/Sept, 1921) 20-1, 39.

Messrs. Duffy, Gill, Hodges & Figgis, Williams & Norgate, Keegan Paul & Co., Constable & Co. and David Nutt. The acting secretaries were requested to obtain estimates from all of them. When the Sub-Committee next met just over a week later, replies had been received from Constable, Gill and Keegan Paul. The others requested further information before replying. No decision had been reached by the meeting of 15 June, the last before the summer recess, and when the committee reconvened on 15 October, the issue was addressed again.

Reference was made at the beginning of the meeting to a *Daily Chronicle* correspondence on the subject of the Irish Texts Society. Part of the 'correspondence' referred to, i. e. a letter from Alfred Nutt of the publishing firm, David Nutt – one of those approached by the ITS Sub-Committee some two months previously – had been reproduced in the August issue of *The Gaelic Journal.* It outlined Nutt's willingness to publish as many volumes as might be required, provided 'Irishmen will engage to subscribe 10s 6d a year for ten years'.[46] The

46 The full text of the letter is:

Sir – In the review of Dr Sigerson's 'Bards of the Gael and Gall' there is a passage to which I should like to take exception on behalf of other publishers as well as on my own. It is stated that 'in the present state of Irish education, the publication of original texts and critical apparatus must be left to learned societies, no publisher being willing, as a rule, to aid individual effort in this direction'. This is not so. Messrs. Teubner, of Leipzig, are publishing at their own risk Holder's 'Old Celtic Thesaurus'; Mr. Niemeyer, of Halle, is publishing, at his own risk, the 'Zeitschrift für celtische Philologie' (the contents of which are chiefly Irish or English); Mr. Hirzel, of Leipzig, is publishing, at his own risk, the series of old Irish texts, with glossaries, apparatus and translations (many in English) edited by Professor Windisch and Dr Whitley Stokes; Messrs. Williams & Norgate have, I believe, published at their own expense, Dr Standish Hayes O'Grady's 'Silva Gadelica'. Lastly, I know that I have published at my own expense a fair number of Gaelic texts (both Irish and Scotch), dating from the earliest period to the present day, with translations and commentaries. I also know that the support accorded to these various publications (with the possible exception of 'Silva Gadelica'), especially from Ireland, is miserably insufficient. And I further know that if there were the slightest chance of any adequate support, I should be perfectly willing to publish as much as any Gael can desire. If 250 Irishmen will engage to subscribe 10s 6d a year for ten years, I will engage to issue during that period from twelve to fifteen volumes of 300 to 400 pages, containing interesting matter adequately edited and translated. It is useless appealing in this country for Government help; it would also seem to be perfectly useless appealing to the great Irish millionaires, although it would be possible to produce a *corpus* of the most valuable old Irish literature at the cost of two or three society functions or a season's shooting. There remains the Irish public, which professes an interest in the national literature. Will it put its hand in its pocket to the extent I have indicated? – Faithfully, Alfred Nutt.

letter was followed by a lengthy reply signed 'mac léighinn', in which the writer, quite accurately, pointed out that 'Mr. Nutt's offer to publish for half-guinea subscribers appears to cover just the same ground as has been already taken up by the Irish Texts Society'. In writing as he did to the *Daily Chronicle*, Alfred Nutt was making an impressive case for his own firm as publishers to the projected Society. However, as is clear from the minutes of the 15 October meeting a decision on the proposal was postponed and, in the meantime, Miss Hull was instructed to communicate with Sealy, Bryers & Walker and with the London Book Depot, 'to enquire on what terms they would print and distribute the volumes of the Irish Text Society, if the committee retained the publishing of the volumes in their own hands'.[47] It is probably significant that the two publishers added to the list here had each published work for Thomas Flannery. It is not clear if the initiative to have them included at this point came from him, as he was not present at the meeting, but it seems likely in the circumstances. As we saw earlier, Nutt and Flannery had already crossed swords in the columns of *The Academy* in 1889 and, as is clear from Flannery's correspondence with David Comyn, a personal animosity appears to have persisted between the two men.[48] In any case, at a meeting on 22 October, estimates having been received from Sealy, Bryers & Walker, a letter from Dr Hyde was read advising the committee to work with Nutt as publisher. Eleanor Hull then proposed, seconded by R. A. Stewart Macalister, that Nutt's offer be considered favourably, and the motion was carried. Negotiation of terms followed over the next few months, and the agree-

47 See also at p. 107 below.

48 Flannery, in a very emotional letter to Comyn, dated 23 August 1897 (MS. 8467, [Comyn], Folder 24, National Library of Ireland) wrote: 'Nutt I distrust and dislike. He is too much the 'Teuton' for me. I have never had anything personal to do with him and I don't think I ever will'. In a postscript to another letter in the same folder, dated 30 August, Flannery enquired of Comyn: 'What is this 'new spec' of Nutt's to which you refer? I must have missed something. I have not read the papers for the last week or two'. This referred, of course, to the *Daily Chronicle* letter. Five days later, having seen the letter, Flannery wrote again to Comyn:

> Nutt's 'idea' then is only our own project – that of the Irish Literary Society - grabbed and put forward as a new and original thing, all out of his own head. It is just like his presumption. I'll have nothing to do with him. There are other London publishers – as Fisher Unwin, Williams & Norgate, Dent, A. Constable and others who would not be unwilling to undertake to bring out Irish texts if a fair number of subscribers could be got – even less than 250. And if texts are to be *ancient* and the whole thing to be merely *archaeological* – I'll have nothing to do with it.

ment between the Society and the publisher was finalised by December.

When the committee met on 15 November, a letter was read from Thomas Flannery resigning his membership of the Text Committee. No reason was given for the resignation, which was accepted 'with very great regret'.[49] Norma Borthwick was instructed to write to Flannery expressing the regret of the committee and thanking him for his promise to edit a text for the Society. There is no evidence other than coincidence to suggest that Flannery's resignation was in any way connected with the acceptance of Nutt as publisher. Flannery appeared to be growing increasingly dejected, and even bitter, in the autumn of 1897, largely, it seems, because of difficulties he was encountering with his projected dictionary.[50] The pessimistic sentiments expressed in this letter are difficult to explain at a time when the ITS project – of which Flannery had been one of the chief instigators – was at a stage more likely to inspire optimism. The two books he referred to in his letter to Comyn, his edition of *Oisín in the Land of*

49 Whatever the significance of this resignation, Flannery was one of those elected to the first Executive Council in April 1898, but thereafter his name only appears on the list of Consultative Council members

50 In his letter of 4 September to David Comyn, criticising Nutt's *Daily Chronicle* piece, he had said:

> Such a fund as I suggest to help in the bringing out of my dictionary would of course be of the greatest practical use and value – and without some such fund my dictionary must be indefinitely put off. I don't believe the Irish Literary Society would take it up officially – though many individual members would help. In the inauguration of any such fund I cannot, of course, take any part. (Ibid.).

In an earlier letter referred to above (note 48), dated 30 August, Flannery had written:

> … Now as to the Dictionary. It will hardly, in any sense, be a 'great' work – the Irish-English part will simply be a school book of some 500 pages, and the second part (English-Irish) still more necessary than the other will be about the same size.
>
> If the Gaelic League or any other body will start a Great Irish Dictionary, in quarto or in 3 or in 6 volumes – let them do so, even if it should take a few years, and I will help them, if they want my help. But my modest work will want no 'editors' and it will be so much my own work that I shall have no scruple at all in calling myself its *author*. At the same time I shall welcome any help I get and gladly acknowledge it. Already I have received contributions and suggestions from Dr Hyde, Fr Hickey, Fr O'Growney and others of my friends, and I need not say that I shall gladly welcome any help and suggestions from yourself.

Youth and *For the Tongue of the Gael*[51] had both been published in 1896. One chapter of the latter book dealt comprehensively with the current state of Irish lexicography, though it made no mention of any ongoing work by the author on a dictionary, and the former contained a notice announcing the imminent appearance of a *Student's Irish Dictionary* 'Being an Irish-English and English-Irish Dictionary for the Use of Schools and Colleges in Two Volumes, each of 500 Pages'. A paragraph announcing the forthcoming dictionary also appeared in the November issue of *The Gaelic Journal*. But the dictionary never materialised. In spite of the claims for its imminent appearance in 1896, Flannery does not appear to have even commenced work on it by 1897,[52] and there is no evidence that he was in any way involved subsequently in the preparation of what became known as Dinneen's Dictionary. Unfortunately, his projected edition of the Life of Saint Colum Cille for the Texts Society was to be doomed also.

The final version of the prospectus first produced early in 1896 was ready for distribution by December 1897. The distribution process employed on this occasion was more efficient than that employed by Flannery. The minutes of the committee meeting for 17 December 1897 include a comprehensive list of the societies to which the

---

> About a publisher and printer there is no difficulty. Professor Cusack of Moorfields, London, who published my *Tír na nÓg* and *Tongue of the Gael* will also publish and print the Dictionary – this is already announced in the former books – what I could not find in all Ireland I found in London. He is willing to do it and able – though he knows he won't make any money by it. The only delay is with myself. The only funds necessary are such as would pay me for my time and labour. The sum already paid me by my publisher is, I find, entirely inadequate. The book must therefore wait and I must get on with it in spare moments only – whilst I earn *bread* in other ways. Writing books for Ireland – *real* Irish books – does not bring a man much bread.
>
> There now, is the whole story, and perhaps you understand it now better than you did before.

51 In Breathnach, Ní Mhurchú, *1882-1982: Beathaisnéis a hAon*, 71 the authors refer to the influence of this book on Padraic Pearse when he received it as a school prize. Pearse does, indeed, refer to the book in a paper entitled 'Gaelic Prose Literature' which he read to the New Ireland Literary Society (of which he was president) in March 1897. He was eighteen years old at the time. See *Collected Works of Padraic H. Pearse: Songs of the Irish Rebels etc.* (Dublin, 1918) 185, 186.

52 It is significant, for example, that all references to the dictionary in Flannery's letter of 30 August are in the future tense!

prospectus was sent. As a result the chairman was able to inform the Inaugural General Meeting in April 1898 that 369 members had joined the Society. The first circulation had only elicited about fifty responses.

When the Provisional Committee had first met in May 1897[53] promises of assistance in the editing of texts had already been received from Hyde, S. H. O'Grady, P. W. Joyce and Comyn. Hyde was the first editor to propose a specific text, namely *Eachtra Ghiolla an Fhiugha,* and his edition of that text was, in fact, the first volume published by the Society though it did not appear as early as was originally intended but in 1899. The next offer to edit a text came in June, from Flannery.[54] It was decided at that same meeting to write to Fr Hickey of Maynooth, B. O'Looney MRIA, Fr O'Leary and others (unspecified) to ask if they would act as editors. In October, O'Looney replied favourably and in December, Comyn wrote, offering to edit Keating's *Foras Feasa.*

On 9 February 1898, Norma Borthwick reported to the committee that Professor Henebry of Washington had in his possession facsimiles of O'Donnell's Life of Colum Cille and that he intended editing the work. A month later she was instructed to write to Flannery to enquire about the progress of his work. He wrote back within days expressing his willingness to resign his work as editor of Manus O'Donnell's Life of Colum Cille in favour of Henebry, if the latter could have his edition ready within the required time. It was then decided to write to Henebry to ask if he would give his edition to the Texts Society when it would be ready. Henebry refused. Meanwhile, the committee was informed that the edition of O'Donnell's Life of Colum Cille which Fr Denis Murphy had been working on at the time of his death was from a fine manuscript in the Franciscan Monastery in Dublin, with which any edition from the Bodleian MS. should be compared. Rev. T. O'Reilly O. S. F wrote to the Society offering to open the Monastery library to any member of the Society who might wish to consult the manuscript used by Fr Murphy. At the last meeting of the Provisional

---

53 The following summary account of the activities of the Provisional Committee (May 1897 – April 1898) is almost entirely based on the minutes of the Committee meetings for the period. For these see Chapter Seven below.

54 Although it is not named in the minutes, the text Flannery was to edit was O'Donnell's Life of Colum Cille.

Committee, five days before the Inaugural General Meeting, a letter was read from Fr O'Growney suggesting to the Society that they produce a handy Irish dictionary. It was decided to reserve the matter for future consideration.

On Tuesday, 26 April 1898, the Inaugural General Meeting of the Irish Texts Society took place in the Rooms of the Irish Literary Society, London. The first chair was taken by R. Barry O'Brien. Then, in accordance with a decision taken at the meeting of the Provisional Committee on the 7th of that month, Goddard Orpen proposed, seconded by J. G. O'Keeffe, that Frederick York Powell be moved to the chair. The most likely purpose of this formality was to signal that henceforth the Irish Texts Society was an autonomous organisation and no longer a sub-committee of the Irish Literary Society. The proposal that Dr Douglas Hyde be asked to accept the post of President of the Society was carried unanimously. Norma Borthwick and Eleanor Hull were appointed Honorary Secretaries and R. A. S. Macalister became Honorary Treasurer. The Executive Council was then elected as follows: Frederick York Powell (Chairman), Goddard Orpen (Vice-Chairman), Alfred Nutt, T. J. Flannery, J. G. O'Keeffe, Daniel Mescal, G. A. Greene, Michael O'Sullivan. Eight Vice-Presidents were elected and the Consultative Council[55] included the names of many of the most distinguished scholars in the field of Celtic Studies, while many others had been invited to serve on that Council.

The work of the Society progressed very rapidly in the first two years of its existence. The Annual Report for the year 1898-9, whilst regretting that the promised first volume – Douglas Hyde's edition of *Giolla an Fhiugha* – had not yet appeared, announced that its appearance was imminent. An additional volume, forming part of an occasional series of older texts – Dr George Henderson's edition of *Fled Bricrend* – was also said to be imminent. Two further volumes were reported to be well advanced, Flannery's *Life of Saint Columkille* (from a manuscript in the Bodleian Library) and Comyn's edition of Keating's *History of Ireland*. Two additional texts had been proposed for publication, one for the occasional series – 'The Fate of the Children of Uisneach' from the Book of Leinster – and a collection of 'hitherto unpublished Munster poetry'. The latter proposal had

55 Also referred to as the Consultative Committee.

come from Fr P. S. Dinneen, and the poems in question were by Aodhagán Ó Rathaille.[56]

Flannery's edition of the Life of Saint Colum Cille had been the subject of considerable discussion during the preceding year, much of it concerning the question of remuneration of the editor. According to the minutes of the Executive Council for 11 July, Flannery undertook to prepare his edition and translation from photographs of the manuscript in the Bodleian Library which the Society agreed to purchase, and to have his work ready to go to press not later than October 1899. However, he did not receive the photographs until November 1898. In March 1899, Eleanor Hull was instructed to write to him in order to be able to report on the progress of his work for the AGM. In a letter to David Comyn soon after this, she expressed the fear 'that Mr. Flannery has done little as yet with his Life of St Columkille'.[57] By April 1900, when the Second AGM of the Society took place, it was possible to report that the first two volumes had been published, namely Hyde's edition of *Giolla an Fhiugha* and Henderson's edition of *Fled Bricrend*. By this time Fr Dinneen's edition of the *Poems of Egan O'Rahilly* was in the press, and both Comyn's edition of Keating's *History* and Mac Neill's edition of the collection of Ossianic poems, *Duanaire Finn*, were reported to be making progress. Flannery's edition of O'Donnell's Life of Colum Cille had still not materialised.

Meanwhile, the suggestion made by Fr O'Growney prior to the Inaugural Meeting of 1898 that the Society produce a 'handy Irish dictionary' had been reconsidered, and the desirablility of such a publication having been agreed to, a sub-committee was appointed in December 1898 to oversee the project.[58] When the question of the dic-

56 In fact, the letter from Dinneen, proposing his edition of Munster poetry 'from mss. of the last 200 years' had been received just prior to the Society's AGM. The letter was read at the meeting of the Executive Council which was held on the same date as the AGM, and the proposal accepted.

57 Ms. 8467 (Comyn), Folder 16, National Library of Ireland. Letter dated 20 April 1899.

58 The members of this sub-committee consisted of: F. York Powell, G. A. Greene, J. G. O'Keeffe, F. A. Fahy, M. O'Sullivan, D. Mescal, Capt. Delahoyde, Dr J. Henry and E. Hull. A special sub-committee was also appointed consisting of F. Collum, T. McSweeney, D. Lehane – all members of the Gaelic League, as Dr Henry was also.

tionary had initially been discussed in the previous July[59] it had been suggested that this work be undertaken separately from the ordinary publications of the Society, with a separate publisher's agreement and special terms to members of the ILS; that assistance should be invited through the columns of *Fáinne an Lae* and other Gaelic papers in collecting any glossaries or other matter that might be available for the use of the compilers; that it should be part of the scheme to follow up the publication of this dictionary by a volume of English-Irish words and that the dictionary should be as small and handy as possible, and contain only modern words. The name of Fr P. O'Leary was proposed as a suitable person to supervise the work – he had already made his glossary of *Séadna* available to the Society.[60] When the dictionary scheme was next discussed, in December, two plans of work were put forward: Daniel Mescal proposed that existing Irish vocabularies be collated and added to from their sources while Dr Henry proposed working from the English-Irish side, translating word for word a small English dictionary. The Chairman was of the same mind as Henry, and the plan finally adopted involved the two systems working concurrently. David Comyn was asked to provide a list of all useful existing glossaries. He produced a long list of titles of published works containing glossaries and added the names of several well known previously published dictionaries.[61]

---

59 In Minutes of the Executive Council meeting of 1 July 1898.

60 In July 1898, *Séadna* had not yet been published as a book; it had appeared in serial form in the columns of the *Gaelic Journal* from November 1894 to April 1897. A second part had been published under the heading 'Gaelic League Publications' in 1898 and the third instalment had appeared in the *Cork Weekly Examiner* between 4 May and 14 September 1901. For a comprehensive account of the publication of *Séadna* see Liam Mac Mathúna's preface to the 1987 edition.

61 The full list, as in the minutes of the Executive Council for 30 December 1898, with further comments by E. Hull (?) within brackets, is as follows:

> 'De Vere Coney's Irish-English Dictionary, Foley's English-Irish Dictionary, Dr Atkinson's edition of Keating's Three Shafts of Death (omitting quotations), P. O'Brien's edition of Keating's Introduction to the Mass, Mr. Comyn's edition of the Díonbhrollach, Dr Joyce's edition of Part I Foras Feasa ar Éirinn, Mr. Comyn's edition of the Youthful Exploits of Finn (modern part), Mr. Flannery's & Comyn's edition of *Tír na n-Óg,* O'Growney's Lessons and Texts ed. by S. P. I. L. (but with caution), Modern version of Cath Ruis na Ríogh, Dr Gallagher's Sermons ed. by Canon Bourke (vocabulary to be used with caution), Catechisms and prayer books'.

To be compared with these works were the following: 'Thady Connellon's English-Irish Dictionary (Paris & Dublin), O'Reilly's Irish-English Dictionary, O'Donovan's Supplement, O'Brien's d[itt]o (infinitives unsafe), Manx & Scottish Gaelic (McAlpin's Dictionaries or MacLeod & Dewar's)'.

Whilst the question of publishing a dictionary was first brought to the attention of the ITS in April 1898 through O'Growney's letter, a correspondence on the subject had been going on for several months prior to that in the columns of *Fáinne an Lae.* It is noteworthy that this correspondence was initiated by Dr William Walsh, Archbishop of Dublin, who in a letter dated 8 January 1898 called for the publication of a Students' Irish Dictionary. Dr Walsh subsequently played an important role in the ITS dictionary scheme by helping to raise funds for the project. He is credited in the Society's Sixth Annual Report (1903-4) with having 'shown from the beginning a constant interest in the dictionary' and the Report then acknowledged that 'in consequence of his support, several of the dioceses have made efforts to raise sums of £20 each to meet his Grace's offer of £20, conditional on the raising of a sum of £400 in amounts of the same value'.[62] On the same page of *Fáinne an Lae* reference is made to a letter signed "J. D." which had appeared in *The Freeman* a week earlier 'appealing

62 The text of Walsh's letter is as follows:

Dear Sir, – I have received the first number of the new weekly, 'Fáinne an Lae', and I have to congratulate you on the successful beginning that you have made. Please put me down as a subscriber.

As I am writing, it occurs to me to ask whether any practical steps are being taken, or are likely to be taken, to bring out a handy Irish-English Dictionary for the use of beginners. I speak of a Dictionary of rather moderate size, like those that are available for the use of beginners in the case of languages such as French, Italian or German.

The vocabularies given at the end of the various Parts of Fr O'Growney's Simple Lessons, and of the various volumes of Irish text that have been published in recent years, are well suited to their purpose. Probably if they were brought together and fused into one, they would not need much supplementing to supply what is required. But each of them is of use only where it is to be found, in connection with the particular book in which it is printed. The result is that a beginner whose knowledge of the words of the language is as yet but limited, is practically shut out from the possibility of taking advantage of many opportunities of making progress that would otherwise be within his reach.

for a well-edited new edition of *O'Reilly's Irish-English Dictionary* at a popular price'. A reply to Dr Walsh's letter, written in Irish, appeared in the following issue of *Fáinne an Lae*; the writer was Norma Borthwick who, while she agreed with the Archbishop on the need for an Irish-English Dictionary, maintained that there was an even greater need for an English-Irish Dictionary. She concluded her letter with a reference to Thomas Flannery's projected dictionary which she hoped to see completed soon.

The next contribution to the discussion consisted of a long letter from Richard Henebry in which the writer proposed that the Irish Texts Society select an English-Irish Dictionary as their introductory volume, anticipating with remarkable accuracy that it might secure the cooperation of Flannery, Comyn and Father O'Leary, 'the great master of purity in phrase and idiom'.[63] One week later, the paper

Take, for instance, your new weekly. In any sentence or paragraph of it there may be a word or two, perhaps some few words, which the beginner cannot as yet make out. If he had at hand a Dictionary of moderate size, such as any schoolboy may have at hand when working at a French lesson, the difficulty could at once be surmounted, and with the extending opportunities of reading that would be gained from week to week, the command of a stock of words sufficient for many ordinary purposes would rapidly be gained.

Perhaps I am wrong in supposing that there is not already in existence such a Dictionary as I contemplate. If there is, I shall be very glad to hear of it.

Would it be possible to utilise a couple of columns of the new weekly for the publication of a practical elementary Dictionary in instalments? I think something of the kind was at least commenced by the late Canon Ulick Bourke many years ago.

With best wishes for the success of the new venture.

I remain, Dear Sir,

Faithfully yours,

William J. Walsh, Archbishop of Dublin.

63 See *Fáinne an Lae*, February 12th 1898, 6.

printed a reply from Comyn which contained much of the information subsequently supplied by him to the Dictionary Sub-Committee.[64] Comyn, too, referred to Flannery's dictionary as if it were a work in progress. The detailed description contained in this letter suggests either that the writer was familiar with the work in question and agreed with Flannery's modus operandi or alternatively that he was familiar

64 Here is the full text of Comyn's informative letter:

Dear Sir, – In a very valuable communication to your sixth number, on the want of an Irish Dictionary, the Rev. Professor Henebry does me the honour of mentioning me as a fit person to co-operate in such a work. Mr. Thomas Flannery, whom he also mentions, has been for some time engaged in the preparation of a Students' Dictionary, both Irish-English and English-Irish. From his philological knowledge and critical acumen, as well as from his familiarity with the living language and his experience in teaching, much is expected by those who know something of his previous work. I believe this expectation will not be disappointed, and that he will produce a Dictionary "on a level with modern standards, simple and exact, for learners."

The Scottish Gael are well provided in this way. Not to speak of the bulky compilations of the Highland Society, or Armstrong, or Shaw, they have MacLeod and Dewar, and MacAlpin, more nearly like what we at present want. The last two named are especially useful as models, and I am sure, with Mr. Flannery's resources, he will be able to produce a better book than either of them. But this is a laborious and slow work, requiring care and time for its completion, more particularly when we consider that it will have a large part in fixing the standard spelling of the language for a future generation. Here I have every confidence in Mr. Flannery's experience and good sense. If he adopts one of several forms of spelling, or prefers one system of inflection to another, I am sure it will not be from habit, prejudice or whim, but that he will in each case be guided by reason, analogy, and the usage of the best modern writers, without, however, a mere servile following of any. I hope he will give under each root word the inflected forms, such as the comparative and plural of adjectives, and of the verb, the "infinitive" (or verbal noun) and, more particularly, of nouns, the endings of the genitive case singular (and plural where it has a special ending), and the forms of the nominative plural. These most useful details are given in no Dictionary but Coney's, a most excellent work, as far as it goes, but requiring to be largely supplemented. Prepared by the then Professor of the Irish language in Trinity College, and intended chiefly for students of the Irish Bible, it travels very little outside the range of their special requirements, and contains few except Scriptural references. Its scope, however, could readily be extended in capable hands, and it would form the nucleus of such a Dictionary as we require. It has been "out of print" for many years, and so is the corresponding work of his successor, Foley, the "English-Irish Dictionary" which is now as hard to be got as O'Begley, the remaining copies having been bought up by the Gaelic Union in 1880, and distributed as prizes to the teachers holding certificates for Irish. O'Donovan's Grammar disappeared at the same time, in the same way.

with the work and felt the lexicographer required specific guidelines. Of course it is possible also that Comyn never saw the work but was merely anticipating what Flannery would produce were he to follow up the ideas he had expressed in *For the Tongue of the Gael*. It is significant that, as in the case of Flannery's own letter on the subject of the projected dictionary, all the references are in the future tense! One further letter appeared in *Fáinne an Lae* on 5 March, from Diarmuid Ó Foghludha, making the case for an English-Irish Dictionary in preference to an Irish-English one.

The Society's Annual Report for the year 1899-1900 noted that 'steady progress' had been made on the compilation of the Dictionary. In February 1901, John Mac Neill was appointed to act as General Editor of the Dictionary,[65] with David Comyn and Fr Peter O'Leary as

---

There has been a great deal done during the past few years. A great deal remains still to do; the work is growing but all will come in time. We must give Mr. Flannery time to compile his Dictionary; such a work cannot be done in a day, nor in a month, and when done, no matter how well, we have Johnson's high authority for saying that the lexicographer, after all, can only hope "to escape reproach". I have myself been engaged, for longer than I care to look back to, on a small book (chiefly for Intermediate students), Keating's "Introduction" (to his History), with translation and full vocabulary. I can honestly say that I have given a great deal of time, care, and thought to its preparation, yet I am not, even now, fully satisfied, notwithstanding the kind assistance of several friends, as to its fitness to face a Gaelic-reading public, which though not so numerous as we could wish, is becoming every year more critical, more exacting, and less easy to satisfy then in the infancy of the movement, when one might rush into print with a light heart. I may mention that I hope to have this little book out by May next, and I am then under *geasa* to the "Irish Text Society" and several private friends, to undertake the editing of the entire text of Keating's History, for which work I have some preparation made, and materials accumulated.

I need hardly say that this will be a heavy work and will, in itself, be sufficient to prevent my active co-operation in Mr. Flannery's undertaking, even if such were needed. But, in any way not inconsistent with these engagements and my allegiance to *Fáinne an Lae* and *The Gaelic Journal*, I shall be glad to help a work I should much wish to see completed - the Students' Gaelic Dictionary. – I am etc, David Comyn.

65 The correspondence dealing with this appointment, consisting of eight letters from Eleanor Hull to John MacNeill, is in the National Library of Ireland, Ms. 10,881, Folder 18. One letter, dated 29. 1. 1901, asking Mac Neill to assume the responsability of sub-editor, is of particular interest for the information it contains on the ongoing work of the Dictionary Sub-Committee, and is reproduced hereunder at pp. 127-30.

assistants, but O'Leary subsequently resigned owing to pressure of work. The Report for the year 1901 announced that the Dictionary would be published by the following Spring, that is, early in 1902.

At the Council meeting held on 12 June 1901, Alfred Nutt pointed out that *Betha Coluimb Cille* was appearing in serial form in the *Zeitschrift für celtische Philologie*;[66] the advisability of proceeding with the text as one of the Society's volumes was then discussed by the Council, and it was decided not to proceed at this time. It was decided to write to Flannery requesting him, at his convenience, to return the photo plates of the manuscript together with the £15 advanced to him in connection with the work.[67] The Council also learned that owing to ill-health, John Mac Neill would be unable to have the Dictionary manuscript ready for the autumn, as planned. It was decided to write to Mac Neill stating that the Society would not press for the manuscript until the Spring, and proposing that he arrange to share the work at his own discretion. The letter written on behalf of the Council by Eleanor Hull is of interest as it mentions Dinneen for the first time as a possible collaborator with the editor if not as actual editor of the Dictionary.[68] However, a reply from Mac Neill, resigning his post as editor, was read

66 Nutt would, of course, have been aware of this as David Nutt, publishers, were the London distributers of the journal. This is not to suggest that there was any ulterior motive on Nutt's part; clearly, Flannery had contributed to his own misfortune by his tardiness in completing the work which he had had on hands since 1898.

67 The advisability of editing this text was discussed again in December. On this occasion Eleanor Hull brought up the matter as she thought that the version published in *ZCP* would not be within reach of the majority of the members. When the matter next came before the Council, in March 1902, it was decided to ask Fr MacErlean to edit the text for the Society.

68 The text of the letter, which is dated June 14th 1901, is as follows:

Dear Mr. Mac Neill,

We were startled at our last Council by Miss Drury's most unexpected announcement that you wished to be relieved of the Dictionary work. I had heard that you were not well and I fear this simply means that you are overworked and want a rest. Would it not be possible to take this? I hoped from what you said that you had been able to devolve some of your other duties in order to have more time for the Dictionary. I am asked to say that if this question is chiefly one of *time*, the date mentioned in the draft agreement was left intentionally vague and that Mr. Nutt would be quite content if the work were done by the Spring and in the publisher's hands, say, in March or April. Then, as regards the devolution of part of the work, we should be perfectly satisfied if you could arrange with Mr. Bergin or anyone else you thought suitable to take off any portion of the work you wished if you cannot continue to supervise. I wrote to Mr. Bergin some time ago to see if he could help in the

at the next Council meeting (17 July). A letter was also read from Comyn offering his services as editor, but in view of the time restrictions imposed by the publisher it was considered that Comyn could not possibly be expected to carry out the task as he already had a volume in hand for the Society. Thus it was decided to write to Fr Dinneen to ask whether he would undertake the General Editorship of the Dictionary. Within six days Dinneen replied stating that, in his opinion, the Dictionary would require a year's steady work and that for practical reasons he could not undertake the task for less remuneration than £250. When the Council met on October 8th, terms were agreed with Fr Dinneen. Alfred Nutt was then authorised to open communications with American firms with a view to printing the Dictionary in America, in order to secure the American copyright. An American edition did not ultimately materialise.

Although the Dictionary occupied much of the Council's time from the latter part of 1901 up to the time of its publication in 1904, other aspects of the Society's work were not neglected, as the Annual Reports for the years 1901-1904 testify. In the first six years of its existence, the ITS published four volumes in addition to the

---

editorial work of the Dictionary as his own had fallen through but he said then that it was impossible as he had not any [word illegible] for Dictionary work. But perhaps he might reply differently to you if you know him personally. *Could* Father Dinneen or Father MacErlean help? The former is working all day at the RIA on his Gaelic League books but he might possibly be able to give his evenings – and we have decided to give up altogether on our edition of Manus O'Donnell's 'Life of Columkille' which we intended to ask Rev. MacErlean to take over from Mr. Flannery as alas! Father Henebry is publishing the work in the current and following numbers of ZCP. This is a great disappointment to us. I do hope your health will admit of your retaining the editorship of the Dictionary but if you can get help we shall be only too glad that you should be relieved as far as possible. Is there anything further that *we* can do to perfect the slips or prepare the work for you? If you find it impossible to go on we must only try to find some other editor, but we should all be truly sorry if this were necessary from every point of view. Still, your health is the first consideration.

Believe me, with truest regards, Eleanor Hull. (Ms. 10,881 (Folder 18), National Library of Ireland).

Dictionary, three other volumes were in preparation by 1904[69] and several further proposals were under consideration.[70] Failure – or threatened failure – by some editors to produce volumes by the promised date constituted a recurring source of anxiety for the Council, and the reputation of the Society as well as the Council's good relations with its editors owed a considerable amount to both the persuasive powers and the diplomatic skills of the Honorary Secretary. Eleanor Hull's persuasiveness and diplomacy probably ensured that the Society's fourth volume (Keating's *Foras Feasa ar Éirinn*, edited by David Comyn) was published in 1902. The Annual Report for 1900-1 stated that 'the Volume for the current year, which is now passing through the press, will contain the first volume of the Society's edition of Keating's *Foras Feasa ar Éirinn* (History of Ireland)'. However, the Annual Report for 1901-2 stated that 'owing to illness, and the heavy nature of the work involved in the comparison of manuscripts, the Editor of the volume for 1901, Keating's 'History of Ireland' has not been able to finish the work within the given time'. It went on to state, however, that the edition was 'now approaching completion, and will be issued immediately'.

The minutes of the Council for 1 October 1901 record a letter from Comyn saying that owing to another attack of illness he had been unable to do any work on his book for some time and that he feared that it could not be ready before the close of the year at the earliest. The Honorary Secretary was directed to urge Mr. Comyn to try to get the volume out within the year and to write to printers to enquire exactly as to the condition and progress of the work. It was decided that no circular such as that proposed by Mr. Comyn notifying subscribers of the delay, should be issued at that time. The minutes for the meeting of 12 December state that, according to Comyn, the text of Keating's History was almost ready for the printers and that he expected to have the translation finished for January. Eleanor Hull then suggested sending the circular to members informing them that the book would not be published that year. At the meeting of 28 January 1902, a letter was read from Comyn stating that the work would not be ready before the end of March. This news prompted a

69 One of these, Agnes Farrelly's edition of *Flight of the Earls* was never published.

70 These included proposals from R. A. S. Macalister, R. Henebry and Fr MacErlean.

lengthy communication from Eleanor Hull, dated 29 January, urging haste with the project for fear that delay might 'injure the Society in the eyes of its members and of the public'.[71]

A week later a letter was read from David Comyn announcing that the work was progressing satisfactorily.[72] The Annual Report for the year 1902-3 stated that the first part of Keating's 'History of Ireland,' edited by Mr. D. Comyn M.R.I.A. had appeared in the previous August and that it was hoped that the editor would be able to complete

---

71 The opening paragraph of the letter shows how seriously the delay in publication was viewed by Council.

> Dear Mr. Comyn,
> You will excuse a serious letter from me. We had a meeting of the Council yesterday at which I was obliged to communicate this unwelcome intelligence that you had now postponed the hope of having the first volume of Keating out till March. Several of our members had confidently reposed upon your former assurance that the book would certainly be in the hands of the public in January at the latest, and the communication was a real blow to their hopes and confidence. You will remember that early in last year you absolutely promised us this book (which was originally to have appeared in January 1901) in October. The arrears are therefore become very serious and following upon the entire[?] failure of Mr. Flannery to keep his engagement to the Council about the volume for last year it is calculated most grave and to injure the Society in the eyes of its members and of the public. Our very existence depends on the regularity with which our publications are issued. We throw ourselves on your honour and on that sense of interest in the welfare of the Society which I am assured that you feel, to accomplish the task that you have undertaken. We feel absolutely bound in honour to produce this complete edition of Keating so long promised to our subscribers. I know it to be the wish of your life to do this work which is in every sense so honourable and worthy a task for the country, and it would cause us infinite regret if the work were not to be brought out under your supervision. The Council, however, feel that if this work is to drag on from month to month as it has been doing this issue of the complete history becomes merely a faint hope and they will not at all feel that their wishes and promises will have been fulfilled by the tardy issue of a mere portion of the whole… (Ms. 8467 (Comyn), Folder 16, National Library of Ireland).

72 Further evidence of Hull's persuasiveness and diplomacy can be seen in her letters to John (Eoin) Mac Neill, one of which is quoted above at n. 68.

the second portion 'at no very distant date'. In fact, the second part (ITS Vol. 8) was not published until 1908; Comyn died in 1907. Part two as well as parts three and four were edited by P. S. Dinneen.[73] This was not the first time Dinneen had agreed to take over from another editor and see his work to a conclusion – he replaced Mac Neill as editor of the Dictionary also, as we saw above.

Fr Dinneen's contribution to the work of the ITS was formidable. In all, he edited (or, as in the case of Keating Vol. 2, partly edited) four volumes for the Society; in addition he took over the editorship of the 1904 edition of the Dictionary, and edited the enlarged 1927 edition as well as the smaller 1910 school edition. His edition of Aodhagán Ó Rathaille's poetry (Vol. 3) was so successful that it quickly sold out and a new edition was published in 1911. There is a certain irony in the fact that when Dinneen first proposed his edition of Ó Rathaille to the Society in April 1899 the Council accepted his proposal but with reservations. They subsequently appointed a sub-committee to report to the General Committee 'on the literary merit of Fr Dinneen's work',[74] and when the Sub-Committee reported back on 1 November, the verdict was that 'generally the readers considered the matter to be of the highest value, the poems being fine in style and substance, but they considered that a considerable revision of the manuscript was necessary as the work was not free from errors of spelling and mistakes in the reading of the original text'. The readers also felt that 'the translation was not always accurate and was frequently verbose and wanting in precision. It was too much hampered by reminiscences of Classical models'.

In fact, the revision of Dinneen's work was a recurring issue for most of the following year.[75] In December it was decided to enlist the expertise of Osborn Bergin, who was then a lecturer in Celtic at Queen's College, Cork, to 'give a final revision to the proofs of Fr

73 In his Preface to *Foras Feasa* Vol. 2, Dinneen explained that:

> Mr. Comyn … while engaged in the preparaton of the second volume, was overtaken by a serious illness, which made it necessary for him to abandon the undertaking. In February, 1907, the present editor reluctantly undertook the completion of the work, as far as text and translation are concerned.

74 The Sub-Committee consisted of D. Mescal, M. O'Sullivan, J. G. O'Keeffe, F. McCollum and T. McSweeney.

75 See the ITS Minutes, Book 1, passim.

Dinneen's "Munster Poems" when ready'.[76] On 2 May 1900 the Council was told that 'very heavy corrections had been made in Fr Dinneen's proofs', and Miss Hull was directed to ask Fr Dinneen 'to have all possible corrections for the future made in the manuscript before sending it to press'. The problems with Dinneen's work were not all over yet. In September the printers wrote to say that Fr Dinneen's volume had exceeded the estimated length by some 100 pages and Mr. Nutt found that he would be unable in this case to publish the volumes at the original figure agreed upon. The book was published before the end of 1900, and the Annual Report for 1900-1 acknowledged the services rendered to the Society by Rev. P. S. Dinneen and by Mr. Osborn Bergin in connection with their edition of O'Rahilly's Poems. Bergin himself did not edit a text for the Society, although apparently he was invited to do so. Mentioning the 'Contention of the Bards' by name, he promised instead to keep the Society in mind when the 'favourable moment' arrived to do some work on it.[77] The text named by Bergin was subsequently edited for the Society (Vols. 20 and 21) by one of his students, Fr Lambert McKenna, who also edited two further volumes of Bardic Poetry (Vols. 37 and 40).

By the early months of 1904, the Dictionary was nearing completion. Dinneen had objected strongly to the suggestion that it be brought out in parts, and the Council finally agreed that it should not.

---

76 Dinneen's biographers claim that he had no formal training as an editor of manuscripts apart from that which he acquired accidently from his fellow Jesuits. See P. Ó Conluain agus D. Ó Céileachair, *An Duinníneach* (Dublin, 1958), 309.

77 In a letter to the Honorary Secretary, dated 4 April 1904, Bergin wrote:

> Dear Miss Hull,
>
> I need not say how much I should like to take up the editorial work you mention. It would be far more satisfactory than looking on and correcting or criticising the work of others. But I have not been in Dublin since the year before last and may not be there for another year. The last time I visited the Academy I collated a portion of the 'Contention of the Bards' of which I have a copy, with two or three mss. But it would take three or four months to do that properly, so it would not be fair for me to make any promise about it yet.
>
> I can only promise not to forget the Society's interests when the favourable moment arrives.
>
> Yours sincerely,
>
> Osborn J. Bergin. (MS. G 567 [item ii, loose documents], National Library of Ireland).

At the Annual General Meeting on 10 May it was announced that the work was completed up to the letter S and that the volume would be ready for August. It was decided at a Council meeting on 28 June that the Dictionary would have a Council's Preface and an editor's Preface. Dinneen concluded his editor's Preface with the following words:

> Although this work was laid on my shoulders quite unexpectedly, it is curious to recall that the production of an Irish Dictionary was one of the dreams of my boyhood. If the realization of that dream be not as splendid as the original conception, it is some compensation to reflect that the work, in spite of many imperfections, will be useful to thousands of students, and will help on the work of cultivating the rich and vigorous, but sadly neglected, language of the Gael.

Dinneen was quite well aware of the limitations of the work he had undertaken and completed. He gave the reasons for these limitations, as he perceived them, in the course of a lengthy reply to Fr M. P. O'Hickey's highly critical review of the Dictionary.[78] The concluding paragraph of Dinneen's response to Hickey, entitled 'Irish Lexicography – A Reply', reveals his own keen awareness of the shortcomings of the work:

> Neither the editor nor the Council of the Irish Texts Society intended to put this book on the market as a work infallibly perfect, or sufficiently full for all purposes.[79] From the nature of the case the work has no pretensions to that practical infallibility which can be attained by works of a similar size in modern highly cultivated languages, works that are but condensations, over and over again

---

78 Both review and reply appeared in *The Irish Ecclesiastical Record*, July 1904, January 1905. On the second last page of his twenty-two page article entitled 'Irish Lexicography' Hickey wrote:

> The Irish Texts Society's Dictionary, be its defects what they may, is a work to be taken seriously. With all its shortcomings, – and they are, as will be seen, neither few nor trivial, – its publication is unquestionably an event of great importance. The gratitude of Irish Ireland, and indeed, of the Irish race, is due to the Society for its patriotic enterprise, and for the tireless energy and devotion with which, in face of many difficulties and discouragements, it clung to its purpose and laboured to the end for the advancement of a great and praiseworthy project. The editor, too, worked hard and tirelessly, but neither his critical knowledge, nor his capacity for taking pains, appears to be on a level with his industry.

79 The project, as originally conceived in July 1898, had been for a dictionary 'as small and handy as possible'. See p. 22 above.

> edited and corrected, of voluminous and encyclopaedic dictionaries, on which treasures were expended, and which it took generations to compile. In the time at the editor's disposal and with his limited assistance, it was utterly impossible for him to ransack the monuments of the language that are still locked up in musty manuscripts, it was impossible for him even to verify at first hand every local word and variant. But though the work is necessarily imperfect in many respects, it is capable of improvement and development. Future editions can be improved by the aid of prudent, well-considered, helpful criticism, but no good result can accrue from the self-imposed work of critics who stand convicted of possessing neither the 'critical knowledge and capacity for taking pains' to be accurate, nor the disposition to be even-handed and just.

The Society did, of course, publish an enlarged edition of the Dictionary, with Dinneen as editor, in 1927.

Council and sub-committee meetings were necessarily frequent and demanding during the first six years of the Society's existence, and the voluntary group of dedicated people who constituted those committees carried out their diverse tasks with both imagination and courage. In this centenary year of the foundation of the Irish Texts Society, one wonders if Frederick York Powell, when he referred to 'matter enough unprinted to keep such a society going for a century' could possibly have envisaged the fifty-nine handsome green volumes (not including the various editions of the Dictionary and the Subsidiary Series) which are the material legacy of the Society's first century. As the Society enters its second century, one wonders if any scholars working in the field of Celtic Studies, or even if any mere amateurs of Irish literature, could possibly envisage a world *without* that legacy.

CHAPTER TWO

The Irish Texts Society and the Development of Irish Language Scholarship

Brian Ó Cuív

With the founding of the Irish Texts Society in 1898 began an enterprise in Irish textual editing and publication whose achievements are unparalleled. Since then we have seen published fifty-nine serial volumes (including vols. 3a and 29a). In addition the Society has in its publication list the two editions of Pádraig Ua Duinnín's *Foclóir Gaedhilge agus Béarla* (1904, 1927, the latter having been reprinted with additions in 1934, and on numerous occasions since then), as well as several items in its Subsidiary Publications Series. A vigorous reprinting programme pursued by the Council in recent years has ensured that all of the volumes and the *Foclóir* will be available for purchase in the centenary year.

It is important to consider the Society's publications against the backgound of other serial publications inaugurated in the last century, such as the Transactions of the Ossianic Society (1854-61), the volumes published by the Irish Archaeological and Celtic Society (1841-80) and the Celtic Society (1847-55), the Royal Irish Academy's Todd Lecture Series (1889-1935), and the literary publications of Cumann Buanchosanta na Gaedhilge from 1883 on. The earliest of these had come at a time when a small number of people began to show an interest in Ireland's literary past. The Academy's publications were not unconnected with the fact that its library contained manuscript sources of great importance and diversity. On the other hand the aim of Cumann Buanchosanta na Gaedhilge in publishing such works as *Oidhe Chloinne Lir* (1883) and *Oidhe Chloinne Tuireann* (1888) was to provide texts for use in schools following the official recognition in 1878 of Irish as a subject in the school curriculum.

The foundation of the Irish Texts Society came five years after the foundation of the Gaelic League in 1893, and although the aims of the two were very different they shared a common desire to promote an interest in Irish literature from manuscript sources. Furthermore two eminent scholars were to make important contributions to both organisations – Douglas Hyde and Patrick Dinneen (Pádraig Ua Duinnín). Indeed Hyde, who edited the first of the Society's volumes which appeared in 1899, had the distinction of being President of both for over twenty years. In addition to volume 1 containing *Giolla an Fhiugha* and *Eachtra Cloinne Rígh na h-Ioruaidhe* he edited volumes 19 (*Gabháltais Shearluis Mhóir*) and 36 (Hull Memorial Volume: *Sgéalta Thomáis Uí Chathasaigh*). Dinneen's first contribution was his edition of *Dánta Aodhagáin Uí Rathaille* which appeared as volume 3 in 1900 and again in a revised version as volume 3a in 1911. His other contributions to the series were volumes 8, 9 and 15 (parts II-IV of Keating's *Foras Feasa ar Éirinn*, the first part having been edited by David Comyn as volume 4 in 1901). However, Dinneen's best-known contribution to the Society was his *Foclóir Gaedhilge agus Béarla* which has been mentioned already and which has been an indispensable tool for Irish scholars over the years. The Irish Texts Society provided a new outlet for the publication of serious works of Irish scholarship, a fact which was important with the increasing interest and activity in the study of Irish at university level, both in Ireland and abroad. Furthermore the establishment of an advisory editorial committee signalled the Society's intention of setting high standards of both scholarship and technical production.

At the time of its foundation it was stated that the Society's work should be 'chiefly directed to the publication of texts in modern Irish'. What was intended, of course, was not contemporary Irish writing, of which there was relatively little in 1898, but texts from manuscript sources which were abundant. The first volume opened to most of its readers a new window on Ireland's literary past. It contained two stories which were typical of the kind of narrative which had delighted audiences in past centuries and which still made Ireland renowned for its folk-literature, *Giolla an Fhiugha* and *Eachtra Cloinne Rígh na h-Ioruaidhe*. The editor, Douglas Hyde, was already recognized as a scholar of standing and for its time his edition was very creditable. It consisted of the texts of the tales, together with manuscript variants, English translation and glossary, all preceded by an introduction in which the editor discussed his manuscript sources and various linguistic features.

At the first Annual General Meeting, which took place before the first volume was published, it was announced that while occupying themselves chiefly with the production of modern texts the Committee proposed to publish occasional extra volumes containing earlier texts of importance. The first of these was *Fled Bricrend*, a tale of the Ulster cycle edited by George Henderson from the twelfth-century manuscript *Lebor na hUidre*. This appeared as volume 2 in 1899 which also saw the publication of volume 1. On the production side these first volumes proved to be attractive ones, well printed and bound in the distinctive green and gold which has been maintained ever since. With the publication of *Fled Bricrend* as the second volume in the series, the idea of denoting some volumes as 'extra volumes' was dropped. From that on the whole range of Irish literature, from late Modern Irish back to Old Irish, both in prose and in verse, was regarded as suitable for the provision of volumes for the Society.

In fact the next volume brought to readers the work of one of the most celebrated of the later Munster poets, Aodhagán Ó Rathaille of Kerry. While copies of his poems were numerous in Irish manuscripts only a few had been published prior to that time. In volume 3 Father Pádraig Ua Duinnín presented forty-six poems which he attributed to him, as well as some prose pieces and a handful of poems by other Munster poets. The poems were accompanied by an English translation and were preceded by an informative introduction on Ua Rathaille's life and times and on other matters, including the metrics of assonantal verse. This was the first time that an attempt had been made to gather together from disparate sources the extant work of an Irish poet and the edition of 750 copies was sold out very quickly and a new edition was put in hand, with Tadhg Ó Donnchadha collaborating with Ua Duinnín as joint editor, and this appeared in 1911. The second edition included the text of documents that were then in the Public Record Office in Dublin and which throw light on the background to Ua Rathaille's life and writings.

In the meantime the first volume in a three-volume edition of the poems of the greatest post-classical Munster poet, David Ó Bruadair, appeared in 1910, with the others following in 1913 and 1917. Ó Bruadair was born about the beginning of the reign of Charles I and died in January 1698, so that he experienced the sufferings and joys of Irishmen over a period of nearly seventy years and his poems provide us with a unique commentary on what he saw and felt. The very large number of them which have survived – there are eighty-eight in Father John MacErlean's edition – is due partly to his own scribal activity and partly to that of his friends and admirers who recognised the qualities of his work and copied and recopied much of it. In the concluding chapter of the introduction to the first volume of his edition Father MacErlean, having referred to the establishment of the Protestant ascendancy under William of Orange, wrote: 'In the consequent decline of Irish learning and culture, David Ó Bruadair was quickly forgotten. His memory, which survived for a while among the broken bands of learned scribes, historians, and poets, was in succeeding generations almost completely eclipsed. Thus passed away into unmerited oblivion one of the greatest masters of Irish style, one of the last of those Irish poets who had been trained in the yet unbroken tradition of the classical poetic schools'. Father MacErlean's edition of Ó Bruadair's verse rescued the poet from the oblivion to which he had been consigned, and I would rate it as one of the most important contributions to an understanding of Irish history from the seventeenth century on.

A year before the last of the Ó Bruadair volumes appeared another collection of later Irish poetry was published. This was *Amhráin Chearbhalláin: The Poems of Carolan* (vol. 17), edited by Tomás Ó Máille, a native Irish speaker from West Galway who had attended classes in the School of Irish Learning in Dublin and had subsequently studied under Kuno Meyer and Rudolf Thurneysen before becoming Professor of Irish in University College, Galway. This volume of 440 pages reflects Ó Máille's versatility, for the range of his scholarship extended from Old Irish to the phonetics of the spoken language. In it he edited 132 poems of the late seventeenth and early eighteenth century, the majority of which were by Carolan. While one might say that the poetry did not reach the high standard of the best of Ó Bruadair's or Ó Rathaille's work, it did relate to the society in which Carolan, poet and harper, found a warm welcome which he repaid with his musical and verse compositions.

All in all the Society made available to readers a considerable amount of earlier Irish poetry. The year 1908 saw the publication of the first part of *Duanaire Finn* (vol. 7) in which Eoin Mac Neill edited 35 of 69 poems of the Fionn cycle preserved in a manuscript written in the Netherlands in 1626-1627. The publication of the text was completed by Gerard Murphy in 1933 (vol. 28), with a final volume in 1953 (vol. 43) which, supplementing the lengthy introduction which Mac Neill had written for his volume, gave us the most comprehensive study ever published of this literary genre.

The serious study of Early Modern Irish bardic poetry had scarcely begun when the Irish Texts Society was founded, although there is evidence that Osborn Bergin was already familiar by then with many of its metrical conventions and had developed an interest in it which was to be very productive and which led him to give a course of lectures on it in the School of Irish Learning in 1914. Among Bergin's pupils were Father Lambert McKenna and Eleanor Knott and it is to them that the Society owes several volumes which established norms of study and editing which have guided scholars over the years. McKenna's work on bardic poetry continued throughout his lifetime and his publications were not confined to the Society volumes which were *Iomarbhágh na bhFileadh*: *The Contention of the Bards* (vols. 20 and 21) published in 1920, and *Aithdioghluim Dána* (vols. 37 and 40) published in 1939/40. These works and Eleanor Knott's masterly edition of *The Bardic Poems of Tadhg Dall Ó Huiginn (1550-1591)* (vols. 22 and 23), which came in 1922 and 1926, have been used by generations of students. Joep Leerssen's *The Contention of the Bards (Iomarbhágh na bhFileadh) and its Place in Irish Political and Literary History*, published as the second of the Society's Subsidiary Series in 1994, and Pádraig A. Breatnach's new introduction to Eleanor Knott's volumes, published in 1996, have added further interest to these scholars' work. Two recent volumes which show the Society's continuing activity in this area must be mentioned here. They are *The Poems of Giolla Brighde Mac Conmidhe* (vol. 51), edited by Nicholas Williams and published in 1980, and *Poems on Marcher Lords* (vol. 53), edited by Anne O'Sullivan and Pádraig Ó Riain and published in 1987.

Before passing on from the subject of poetry there is one more volume which calls for special attention. This is *The Poems of Blathmac Son of Cú Brettan* (vol. 47) edited by James Carney and published in 1964. Included along with Blathmac's verse are an Old Irish poem based on the apocryphal Gospel of Thomas and another one on the Virgin Mary. This fascinating body of early verse had lain unnoticed for many years in a seventeenth-century manuscript in the National Library of Ireland until Carney brought it to the attention of the public and subsequently published it in the Society's edition. In the four poems we have twelve hundred lines of verse which are a welcome addition to known literary texts from the Old Irish period, predating as they apparently do *Félire Oengusso* by at least some decades.

Many categories of text are represented in the corpus of prose works published by the Society. These include tales which are illustrative of the various Irish tale-cycles or which come from the classical or medieval European tradition, works relating to Irish history or prehistory, religious works, including saints' lives, and scientific works. Two of the volumes containing tales have been mentioned already. An edition of the second of these, *Fled Bricrend*, had been published in Germany in 1880, but Henderson's edition, which, as the Society's policy required, had an English translation, made the tale more accessible and gave readers some idea of the nature of the heroic cycle of Ulster tales. Two later volumes showed the development of the cycle in the late medieval period under the influence of a more romantic tradition. These are *Caithréim Conghail Chláiringhnigh* (vol. 5) edited by P. MacSweeney, and *The Pursuit of Gruaidh Grian-Sholus* (vol. 24) edited by Cecile O'Rahilly whose *Táin Bó Cúalnge* (vol. 49), edited with great expertise from the Book of Leinster, gave us this twelfth-century recension of the most central of the Ulster tales. The publication in 1992 of Caoimhín Mac Giolla Léith's *Oidheadh Chloinne hUisneach* (vol. 56) brought us an Early Modern Irish version of the best-known of the *réamhscéalta* or foretales of the *Táin*.

The mythological and Fionn cycles are represented in the series by one tale each: *Cath Maige Tuired* (vol. 52) and *Tóruigheacht Dhiarmada agus Ghráinne* (vol. 48). The first of these goes back linguistically to the Old Irish period but has survived only in a sixteenth-century manuscript, while the second is probably the best-loved of the Fionn tales and achieved immense popularity in the Early Modern Irish period and later. These modern editions – the first by Elizabeth A. Gray and the second by Nessa Ní Shéaghdha – are particularly welcome. From the so-called 'historical cycles' we have *Buile Suibhne* (vol. 12) and *Cath Maige Mucrama* (vol. 50). The first of these, which was edited by J. G. O'Keeffe, is one of three late Middle Irish tales based on historic events surrounding the battle of Mag Rath in the seventh century. The other two had been edited by John O'Donovan as far back as 1842, but it fell to O'Keeffe to bring readers the story of Suibhne who is associated in the Irish story with Saint Moling and about whom traditions were current in the Old Irish period. In a new introduction which he wrote for the reprint edition of Vol. 12, also published separately as Subsidiary Series 4, Professor Joseph Falaky Nagy considered various scholarly explorations of the story of Suibhne over a period of more than sixty years and presented a fresh analysis of the tale and of the significance of elements in it.

Volume 50 contains four stories derived from Munster traditions of the pre-historic period and transmitted in late Old Irish or Early Middle Irish, edited in exemplary fashion by Máirín O Daly.

Imtheachta Aeniasa: The Irish Aeneid (vol. 6), edited by George Calder, provided an interesting example of a medieval Irish writer's attempt to convey in prose form the story told in Vergil's *Aeneid*, the Latin text of which is believed to have been used by the adaptor. Erich Poppe's new introduction to this volume (Subsidiary Series 3, 1995) is a very useful contribution to our knowledge and understanding of the treatment in medieval Ireland of the classical literature of Greece and Rome. Unlike the story of Aeneas the version of the Hercules story found in Gordon Quin's excellent edition of *Stair Ercuil ocus a Bás* (vol. 38) is almost certainly based on Caxton's fifteenth-century English version of Raoul Lefevre's *Recueil des Histoires de Troyes*. A slightly earlier text from European tradition is *Gabhháltais Shearluis Mhóir* (vol. 19) which its editor, Douglas Hyde, believed was adapted from a Latin original composed in the eleventh or twelfth century. Finally medieval Arthurian storytelling is represented by *Two Irish Arthurian Romances* (vol. 10) published in 1908 and edited by R. A. S. Macalister. This volume is very different from the others discussed above. Apart from the Irish text and English translation it contains very little in the way of editorial analysis or comment. In his short introduction Macalister, who as a professional archaeologist was Director of Excavations in Palestine, explained this by saying: 'But a few days snatched from an interval between two foreign sojourns, each several years long, was all I was able to devote to work on the Manuscript materials: it was in that short time impossible to do more than transcribe, as rapidly as possible consistent with due care, one version of each text, and to glance cursorily through the others'. A devastating but fully justified review by Tomás Ó Rathaille, published in *Irisleabhar na Gaedhilge* in 1909 concluded with this comment: 'The very mildest thing that can be said of Mr. Macalister's book is that it is thoroughly unsatisfactory; and one cannot but regret that the time and money spent upon it were not employed to better advantage'.

Seven years before that the Council of the Society had accepted an offer by Macalister to edit for them *Lebor Gabála Érenn* (the 'Book of the Taking of Ireland', sometimes called the 'Book of Invasions'), the supposed traditional account, in prose and verse, of the settlement of Ireland in pre-historic times and of the establishment of the Goidels – the descendants of Míl Espáine – as the dominant power. In fact it was 1938 before the first part of *Lebor Gabála Érenn* (vol. 34) was published, with further parts following in vols. 35, 39, 41, and 44. While this elaborate and complicated edition has some useful elements, its many defects were pointed out in critical reviews which have been referred to in the new introduction written by John Carey for the recent reprint of vol. 34. While the unfortunate truth is that Macalister was not a competent editor of Irish texts Carey's final comment is worth quoting: 'All those who study LGÉ have benefited from his titanic undertaking, and will continue to do so in the years ahead'.

In his foreword to the 1987 reprint edition of *Foras Feasa ar Éirinn* (vols. 4, 8, 9 and 15) Breandán Ó Buachalla discussed Keating's work in the context of seventeenth-century historiography. In the *díonbhrollach* to the *Foras Feasa* Keating himself set down the motivation for his work, which was to counter false and misleading statements about Ireland and its inhabitants made by authors down the ages. The two books of the *Foras Feasa* contain a continuous narrative of Irish history from the earliest times down to the twelfth century. As source material for the first part Keating used the traditional account as found in *Lebor Gabála Érenn*. As a framework for the later stages he used the regnal list found in the tract *Do Fhlaithesaib Érenn* in the Book of Leinster and other manuscripts, and he supplemented this from a variety of sources, such as tales, anecdotes, saints' lives, and even Giraldus Cambrensis's *Expugnatio Hibernica* which he used for his account of the Anglo-Norman invasion. Keating's work had a wide circulation in manuscript form and for over two hundred years it was the main popular source of knowledge about Ireland's remote past. David Comyn and Pádraig Ua Duinnín performed a signal service in making the Irish text available to modern readers. To Ua Duinnín must be given the credit for rounding off the work with the volume containing the genealogies and index, the compilation of which was a tedious and time-consuming task.

Contemporary with Keating was Lughaidh Ó Cléirigh who contributed four poems to the 'Contention of the Bards' (ITS vol. 20, poems IV, VI, VII and IX). In these he showed himself to be accomplished in the use of the bardic language and metres. However he is probably better known as the author of *Beatha Aodha Ruaidh Uí Dhomhnaill* (vols. 42 and 45) and for it he chose to adopt an artificial archaising style which is unattractive and tedious to read. Unlike Keating's *Foras Feasa*, which was copied and recopied, the *Beatha* has survived in a single manuscript from which it was first edited by Rev. Denis Murphy in 1893. This edition was far from satisfactory and Father Paul Walsh undertook to provide a new one for the Society. Unfortunately his death in 1941 brought his work on it to an end and his friend Colm O Lochlainn took on the task of completing the edition. In a foreword to volume 45 he explained the background to the Society's edition of the *Beatha,* including the fact that in the absence of a new translation by Walsh he had printed Murphy's translation, incorporating in it some corrections made by Walsh in his copy of the 1893 book. The Irish text and the translation appeared in volume 42. The additional volume contains not only a lengthy introduction which incorporated work by Walsh and a very full glossary compiled by Máirín O Daly but also a great deal of material which, while not directly connected with Lughaidh Ó Cléirigh's work, is interesting. O Lochlainn's task in handling Walsh's unfinished work was difficult and he recognized that as presented it had many blemishes. He was, as he said 'a working printer' who had undertaken the task 'with overmuch zeal and piety'. Nevertheless he did give us this edition of a unique account of one of the most famous of the northern chieftains of Elizabethan times.

Lebor na Cert is another work which had been published previously. It purports to record the rights of the king of Ireland, the provincial kings, and the tribal kings within the provinces, as well as the stipends due from the higher kings to those below them. John O'Donovan, whose elaborate edition of it from the Book of Lecan was issued by the Celtic Society in 1847, accepted it as an authoritative source for the study of Irish history, a tenth-century document based on much earlier sources. More than two centuries earlier Keating had cited it as a reliable source but he was criticised for doing so by a grandson of Lughaidh Ó Cléirigh who wrote of it: *is dísle Leabhar na nÉcceart do ghairm de iná Leabhar na cCeart* 'it were more proper to call it the Book of Wrongs than the Book of Rights'.[80] Eoin Mac Neill, who discussed the work in 1919, remarked: 'A new edition is very much to be desired, with a critical treatment of the text and more accurate notes, taking advantage of the great increase of philological,

80 *Éigse* 11, 135.

historical, and topographical knowledge accumulated during the seventy years that have passed since this first and only edition was brought out'.[81] Other scholars, including T. F. O'Rahilly and D. A. Binchy, cast doubt on the antiquity of the Book of Rights and Myles Dillon published an assessment of it in 1958.[82] Dillon followed this with the very welcome critical edition of the text which was published by the Society as volume 46 in 1962. By making this new edition available he performed a notable service to Irish studies, for even if the text is of less importance to historians than was thought in the past, it is full of interest and can still provide scope for further scholarship.

Caithréim Thoirdhealbhaigh (vols. 26 and 27), edited by Standish Hayes O'Grady, is unique among the Society's publications in as much as it had been prepared and most of it printed for publication by Cambridge University Press at the time of O'Grady's death in 1915 but remained unpublished until the Irish Texts Society took it over and put the completion of the edition in the hands of Robin Flower who also carried on O'Grady's work of cataloguing the Irish manuscripts in the British Museum. The *Caithréim*, which is probably the work of a professional poet-historian writing in the interests of the branch of the O'Briens represented by Toirdhealbhach Ua Briain (+1268) and his sons, is a stirring account of dynastic conflict in Thomond in the thirteenth and fourteenth centuries and of O'Brien resistance to the advance in that region of Anglo-Norman power under members of the de Clare family. Its importance as a historical source was recognized over a century ago by T. J. Westropp, and in making the text and translation available in 1929 the Society facilitated the work of more recent scholars in following the complicated course of events in north Munster in the two centuries after the coming of the Anglo-Normans.

In the wake of the Anglo-Norman invasion came new contacts with Britain and continental Europe which in turn led to an increase in the production of translation literature. Mention has already been made of some tales derived from external sources. But there was also considerable activity in the realms of scientific, philosophical and religious writing. Although much of this is still unfortunately unpublished, the Irish Texts Society did not ignore its existence. *An Irish Astronomical Tract* (volume 14), edited by Maura Power at the suggestion of Osborn Bergin whose advice and assistance she had in the course of

81 *Phases of Irish History* (Dublin, 1919) 276-7.
82 *Celtica* 4 (1958) 239-49.

her work, is an adaptation of a Latin version of a work by the eighth-century Arabic astronomer Messahalah of Alexandria.

Rosa Anglica (vol. 25), edited by Winifred Wulff who attained a considerable knowledge of Irish medical literature in translation from her work on manuscripts in the Royal Irish Academy, is based on a medical work by John of Gaddesden who studied in Oxford in the fourteenth century, became Court Physician to Edward II, and died in 1361. In addition to the Irish text, English translation, technical vocabulary, and indexes, the volume contains a long introduction in which the editor discusses such matters as hereditary physicians in Ireland, Scotland and Wales, and Irish medical manuscripts in libraries in Ireland and Britain.

The announcement that *Instructio Pie Vivendi et Superna Meditandi*, described by Robin Flower as 'a treatise on the monastic life addressed by a spiritual advisor to a nun',[83] was in course of preparation by Rev. John MacKechnie for publication in two volumes was made at the Annual General Meeting in 1933. Both volumes were designated as volume 29, the first, containing the Latin original and fifteenth-century Irish translation, being issued in 1934, and the second, containing an English translation of the Irish text and a very brief introduction, in 1946. Although the work was of some importance as a specimen of the genre of writing to which it belonged it was possibly the dullest of the Society's publications.

New Testament apocrypha have been of special interest to scholars in fairly recent years. In fact as far back as 1925 Robin Flower was working on a volume for the Society in which he planned to publish several apocryphal texts, including versions in Irish of the 'Harrowing of Hell' and the 'Assumption of the Blessed Virgin'. However, the work was not completed and it was 1991 before the Society published one of the medieval apocryphal texts. This was *Stair Nicoméid*: *The Irish Gospel of Nicodemus* (volume 55) edited by Ian Hughes. The Irish text comprises translations of two Latin texts, *Gesta Pilati* and *Descensus Christi ad Inferos* and is a good specimen of this type of writing which was popular in Ireland from about the twelfth century on. In his edition Dr Hughes has given three Irish versions together with translation, commentary and notes, and in a comprehensive intro-

83 R. Flower, *Catalogue of Irish Manuscripts in the British Museum* 2 (London, 1926) 551.

duction he has discussed in a very thorough way the complicated relationship of the extant Irish versions with one another and with the Latin sources, as well as discussing linguistic features in the Irish texts.

The years 1936 and 1937 saw the publication, in volumes 30-33, of a highly original work which is of great interest as reflecting life in a rural part of Ireland in the second quarter of the nineteenth century. This is *Cinnlae Amhlaoibh Uí Shúileabháin*, a diary written by Humphrey O'Sullivan, a Kerry-born schoolteacher living in Callan in County Kilkenny. O'Sullivan was born in 1780 and died in 1837, and in his diary, which covers the years from 1827 to 1835, he recorded details about the weather, flora and fauna, games and pastimes, personal matters, local customs, people and events, including events at national and international level. All in all this is a valuable document for the social history of the time, for it is full of observations on commonplace matters which so often went unnoticed. O'Sullivan followed political matters with interest and in the final volume there is a short speech which he made in Irish calling for unity of purpose in seeking catholic emancipation. The 'diary' and other works by O'Sullivan were edited by Michael McGrath who provided valuable indexes of botanical terms and general vocabulary.

In the introduction to *Life of St. Declan of Ardmore and Life of St. Mochuda of Lismore* (volume 16), published in 1914, Father Patrick Power wrote: 'A most distinctive class of ancient Irish literature, and probably the class that is least popularly familiar, is the hagiographical', and he went on to discuss the genre as seen in the Latin and Irish lives of saints. Four major manuscript collections of lives in Latin were known in the seventeenth century when the Franciscan John Colgan undertook his hagiological researches. Manuscripts containing lives in Irish included the Book of Mac Carthaigh Riabhach, otherwise known as the Book of Lismore, and the manuscript which is now in the Bodleian Library in Oxford where it is designated as MS. Rawlinson B. 512. It fell to Míchéal Ó Cléirigh and contemporaries of his such as Domhnall Ó Duinnín to attempt to maintain the corpus of such material by making copies from earlier manuscripts which were still available, and their example was followed in the eighteenth century. For instance the edition of the life of St. Declan published by Power is based on a copy made from a sixteenth-century manuscript by Ó Cléirigh, while his version of the life of St. Mochuda is based on a manuscript written by Seán na Ráithíneach Ó Murchadha between

1740 and 1750. Power's volume was a welcome extension of the range of material in Irish being provided for members of the Society and the public in general. The publication in recent years of *Betha Adamnáin*: *The Irish Life of Adamnán* (vol. 54), edited by Máire Herbert and Pádraig Ó Riain, and *Beatha Bharra, Saint Finbarr of Cork: The Complete Life* (vol. 57), edited by Pádraig Ó Riain, has illustrated the diversity and the complexity of Irish hagiographical tradition. The publication of Pádraig Ó Riain's monograph *The Making of a Saint: Finbarr of Cork 600-1200* as no. 5 in the Subsidiary Series marks a new initiative on the part of the Society.

In this survey of the work of the Irish Texts Society, in which I have tried to show the great diversity of material it has published, I have referred to a work planned by Robin Flower which did not materialise. Over the years the Society had similar disappointments in the case of other works promised by various well-known scholars, including editions of Tadhg Ó Cianáin's 'Flight of the Earls' by Agnes O'Farelly (see Annual Report for 1905), 'The Poem Book of Hugh MacShane O'Byrne' by J. H. Lloyd (Report for 1908), 'The Poem-Book of the O'Neills of Clandeboy' by Tadhg Ó Donnchadha (Report for 1913 where it was stated that a special donation to the expenses of publication of this volume had been received from His Excellency the O'Neill of Lisbon), a collection of tales told by Tomás Ó Criomhthainn, to be entitled 'The Great Blasket', by Robin Flower (Report for 1926), Irish versions of tales by the Spanish author Montalvan by Thomas F. O'Rahilly (Report for 1931) who was later replaced as editor of this volume by Éamonn O'Toole (Report for 1936), '*Hortus Sanitatis Hibernicus*' by Winifred Wulff (Report for 1935), 'Medieval Irish Philosophic Texts' by Francis Shaw (Report for 1936), and 'Páirlemint Chloinne Tomáis' by H. R. McAdoo (Report for 1940). Any of these works would have been a welcome addition to the Society's publications, and one can imagine the feelings of frustration of Council members at being disappointed on so many occasions, particularly in the case of works which had reached proof-stage, as happened more than once. We must feel grateful to successive officers of the Society, and especially to the Honorary Secretaries and Honorary Treasurers who had to contend with the many problems arising from time to time in their efforts to maintain a schedule of publications. The distinctive volumes in green and gold binding on shelves throughout the world are a lasting testimony to their achievement.

CHAPTER THREE

The Irish Texts Subsidiary Series

Neil Buttimer

A short statement is required to place this series in its appropriate context. The principal objective of the Irish Texts Society (ITS) under whose imprint it appears is to publish editions of works in various domains of Gaelic literature and culture. The Society has done so with distinction during the first one hundred years of its existence. Its fifty-nine titles reflect many aspects of Irish civilisation from the medieval period to the twentieth century. ITS is primarily a voluntary organisation dependent on subscriptions for its income. This fact makes the achievement all the more remarkable. Its output is mainly, although not exclusively, directed at a scholarly readership. Such circumstances mean that print runs have been limited. Consequently, over the course of time quite a few of the Society's volumes became virtually unobtainable. By the 1970s, for example, the keenest of collectors were hard put to locate copies of classics like Eleanor Knott's edition of *The Bardic Poems of Tadhg Dall Ó hUiginn (1550-1591)* (vols. 22 and 23 [1922, 1926]). This is not only a landmark in the presentation and annotation of Early Modern syllabic verse, as Professor Pádraig A. Breatnach recalls in a preface to the 1996 reissue, but also a valuable window on politics and society in the composer's late sixteenth-century Connacht and Ulster. Sightings of *Duanaire Finn* III (vol. 43 [1953]) were rare too. Gerard Murphy's commentary on a large seventeenth-century corpus of Fiannaíocht poetry, its possible origins and linkages, offers a perspective on written and oral tradition as well as their interaction spanning the greater part of two millennia.

The Society's decision in the early 1990s gradually to republish its out-of-print matter was therefore applauded by all who wished to fill gaps in their holdings. The ITS were not alone in their undertaking. The Dublin Institute for Advanced Studies' School of Celtic Studies has also replicated a considerable amount of its stock. This reprinting strategy acknowledges certain incontrovertible realities within the world of Irish studies. Advances in understanding often make it desirable that new editions of the writings in question be attempted. The number of researchers is so small, however, when compared with the extent of the patrimony they are exploring that second, not to mention third or fourth, re-workings of texts are prominent exceptions rather than the rule. All republishing efforts are to be welcomed for one further significant reason. They give ready and renewed access to editions which are now the standard reference-points for entries in dictionaries or debate in books and academic papers.

One step taken by the ITS distinguishes its reprinting enterprise from other similar exercises. This is the publication, simultaneously with many of the reissued works, of independent monographs, most of which describe the titles being brought out again and sketch how the subject-matter represented in them is currently interpreted in contrast to when they were edited, generally some decades ago. There are indications that the items we are discussing became a series by chance only. The sequence of works seems since to have taken on a life and direction of its own. Thus the first, Dr John Carey's *A New Introduction to Lebor Gabála Érenn* (1993) does not bear the sub-title 'Irish Texts Society Subsidiary Series' carried by all its successors. Professor Pádraig Ó Riain's *The Making of a Saint: Finbarr of Cork 600-1200* (Subsidiary Series 5, 1997) provides additional information regarding his *Beatha Bharra,* published in the main series (vol. 47). The latter is not an ITS reprint as such but a new critical edition of the life of Cork's patron saint which initially appeared as recently as 1994. Dr Diarmuid Ó Murchadha's *The Annals of Tigernach: Index of Names* (Subsidiary Series 6, 1997) is a companion to the medieval historical compilation the celebrated Celtic scholar Whitley Stokes edited during 1895-7 in the now defunct and well-nigh inaccessible *Revue Celtique* rather than under the aegis of ITS. The Subsidiary Series is thus varied by nature and has not sought to impose a corresponding uniformity of approach on its contributors. Other aspects of its diversity will become apparent when the titles themselves are examined individually below. This exploration also reveals points at which a reader might differ with their authors regarding arguments put forward or seek amplification of proposals made. Having said as much, the stimulating nature of each of the volumes to hand must be credited with prompting one to think afresh about the topics their expert writers so engagingly investigate.

Carey's publication deals with the background to and production of the most sizeable set of items in the Society's repertory, namely R. A.

S. Macalister's five-part edition of the largely pre-Norman work commonly known in English under the heading the 'Book of Invasions' (vols. 34 [1938], 35 [1939], 39 [1940], 41 [1941] and 44 [1956]). This account of the origin of the early Irish people is not in terms of a Celtic society as that concept is now commonly understood. The text traces the community's formation from the creation story told in Genesis, reflecting the world-view introduced to Ireland on the arrival of Christianity. Carey explores central aspects of this question in his own newly-published *King of Mysteries*.[84] Assessing the balance between external and indigenous elements given expression within this and related narratives is the source of much debate in Irish scholarship at present. The central position *Lebor Gabála* and its doctrines came to occupy in medieval Ireland's self-description gives the discussion added impetus. Carey traces the compilation's development in Gaelic writing down to the seventeenth century, outlines scholarly analysis of it from the early 1800s onwards, and sketches the protracted gestation of Macalister's project from when it was first mooted around 1902 to the last part's posthumous appearance over fifty years later. Macalister grappled with a language of which he was not fully a master and tackled a highly complicated codicological tradition. The monograph examined here acknowledges the edition's resultant defects but highlights its genuine strengths, particularly Macalister's efforts in producing a comprehensive overview of the work's evolution in manuscript. This attempt is unlikely to be repeated in any further single setting.

Identity of another kind is at issue in Professor Joep Leerssen's *The Contention of the Bards (Iomarbhágh na bhFileadh) and its Place in Irish Political and Literary History* (Subsidiary Series 2, 1994). This is an introductory essay to the reprint of the verse collection Rev. Lambert McKenna first published with the Society towards the start of the century (vols 20 and 21 [1920]). The curiously-titled 'Contention of the Bards' was an argument among groups of Gaelic poets in the early 1600s as to which was superior, the southern half of Ireland or its northern counterpart. The anthology's thirty or so compositions seem on the surface to represent an arcane squabble, particularly in

84 J. Carey, *King of Mysteries: Early Irish Religious Writings* (Dublin, 1998).

light of their appeal to ostensibly out-moded precedent or past greatness. Leerssen suggests that they reflect genuine conflict in matters of loyalty and vision of the future between literati from county Clare, such as the poet Tadhg mac Dáire Mheic Bhruaideadha, and his learned contemporaries from elsewhere in Ireland. Tadhg's Protestant O'Brien patrons had reached an accomodation with the English administration. Members of other poetic families, for instance Mac an Bhaird, were arguably more comfortable with the anti-authoritarian stance of the northern O'Neills and O'Donnells according to this volume. Even if other commentators may view matters differently to him,[85] Leerssen's opinions have come to occupy an important place in the debate on the growth and acceptability in the early seventeenth century of political allegiances like Jacobitism. Such is the extent of this scholar's focus on the 'Contention's' contents and import that there is little scope for an assessment of the edition itself. It was, nevertheless, one of McKenna's early extended productions in a lengthy career as a presenter of bardic verse. The existence of a considerable number of eighteenth- and early nineteenth-century versions of the anthology point to other potentially fruitful areas of textual and contextual investigation.

In his *A New Introduction to Imtheachta Aeniasa, the Irish Aeneid* (Subsidiary Series 3, 1995), Professor Erich Poppe considers the Irish adaptation of Vergil's epic story of Rome's establishment when introducing the reprint of Rev. George Calder's edition (vol. 6 [1907]). He traces the life of this productive but little-known Scottish minister, and lists manuscript sources for the work which became available since the Scotsman's time besides the great late fourteenth-/early fifteenth-century Connacht codex, the Book of Ballymote (BB), Calder employed for his copy. Poppe re-examines BB, underlining the fact that the text, largely derived from Vergil, occurs there together with stories of the destruction of Troy, the wanderings of Odysseus and the later career of Alexander the Great. This leads him to suggest that the whole series reflects the manuscript compilers' primary (and somewhat scholarly) concern with these compositions as a repository of information on ancient history. The latter argument tends to overlook a possibility associated with classical recastings generally,

85 See B. Ó Buachalla, *Aisling Ghéar: na Stíobhartaigh agus an tAos Léinn* (Baile Átha Cliath, 1996) 667 n. 80.

and Vergilian specifically, namely their susceptibility to reinterpretation at the time of rewriting or recopying. Jan M. Ziolkowski's introduction to Domenico Comparetti's well-known *Vergil in the Middle Ages* has once more reminded us of the issue of Vergil's contemporary relevance.[86] Here the key to a further appreciation of Calder's volume may lie not so much within BB exclusively as in the broader milieu in which the latter document itself was completed. BB and other contemporary codices from the West of Ireland (not to mention their impressive Munster counterparts) belong to an era witnessing the ebb and flow of energies and empires, the relative decline in the fortunes of the Norman colony coupled with a resurgence in Gaelic self-confidence to which the actual drafting of the manuscripts in question tellingly attests. Interest in the classical works mentioned here may betoken a real-life concern with seeking guidance from the tale of Rome's foundation and regeneration (and from the other aforementioned works) regarding the advantages and hazards that radical changes in the political order present. The altered circumstances of later medieval Ireland may have brought about a corresponding set of opportunities and challenges in the domestic sphere, however temporary these possibilities turned out to be.

Departure, albeit of a different type, is a feature of the famous legend about the deranged seventh-century ruler Suibhne mac Colmáin Chuair which J. G. O'Keeffe edited for the Society (vol. 12, [1913]). Professor Joseph F. Nagy reconsiders this work in his *A New Introduction to Buile Suibhne (The Frenzy of Suibhne)* (Subsidiary Series 4, 1996). The tale relates how and why Suibhne went mad, left his territory and people to wander throughout Ireland, volubly expressed his sense of alienation, failed repeatedly to be rehabilitated but was finally reconciled only at the moment of his violent death. Nagy outlines theories of the saga's provenance, particularly competing views as to the native or foreign derivation of some of its elements. His principal concern is to examine Suibhne himself and the story as a whole as exemplars of traditions about eloquent marginalised figures in Irish culture. This theme was previously treated in the author's well-known study *The Wisdom of the Outlaw.*[87] Nagy's Subsidiary

86 Original edition 1885, new edition, Princeton, 1997.

87 J. F. Nagy, *The Wisdom of the Outlaw: the Boyhood Deeds of Finn in Gaelic Narrative Tradition* (Berkeley, Los Angeles, London, 1985)

Series monograph partially anticipates a subsequent publication of his, *Conversing with Ancients and Angels*,[88] by also focussing on clerical motivation for recording and perpetuating stories principally concerned with the affairs of secular personalities. While acknowledging Nagy's sociological, anthropological and literary insights, one wonders whether there may not yet be much to unfold regarding the psychological elements to Suibhne's personal experience and that of his complex interaction with the wider community. The lengthiest version of the mad king's saga is found in a seventeenth-century source completed one thousand years after its principal actor's lifetime. Further analysis of this and related documents might also illuminate the issue of the story's shaping and reception in later periods.

Saints play a particular part in Suibhne's banishment and reconciliation, a fact which illustrates their key power-brokering and mediating function in Gaelic culture at large. No one scholar has done more in recent years to clarify the hagiographical dimension to the Irish past than Pádraig Ó Riain, editor of the aforementioned Life of Finbarr of Cork and current President of ITS. His edition is the most comprehensive assemblage to date of materials in Latin and the vernacular relating to any Irish saint. The volume mainly traces the textual development of the Finbarr biography together with its employment for devotional and liturgical purposes. His Subsidiary Series publication noted earlier focusses on the secular and ecclesiastical background to the legend, particularly employment of the life in furthering the expansionary ambitions of the late twelfth-century diocese of Cork. Ó Riain's study encourages one to speculate on other possible usages of the composition, this time chiefly in the temporal domain. The earliest Irish-language version of the biography occurs in the fifteenth-century Book of Fermoy, completed for members of the Gaelicised Welsh-Norman family, the Roches. It is found there together with the Lives of other diocesan founder-figures like Carthach of Lismore. This fact may indicate inquisitiveness on the part of recent settlers in the north Cork and mid-Munster region generally surrounding the background to ecclesiastical administrative and other structures within their new area of activity.

88 J. F. Nagy, *Conversing with Ancients and Angels: Literary Myths of Medieval Ireland* (Ithaca and London, 1997).

Although last in the series, Diarmuid Ó Murchadha's index of the Annals of Tigernach, also spoken of earlier, is the lengthiest to date at over two hundred pages. This is a painstaking inventory of the personal, place and tribal names of Ireland, complemented by two shorter personal, place and people listings for overseas biblical, classical and Roman references found within one of the premier sets of medieval Irish annals. Ó Murchadha summarises the background and textual history of, as well as scholarly commentary on, this compilation. He proceeds to explain his indexing policy with regard to issues like dating, spelling conventions and the like. Whitley Stokes, as stated, published these annals in a relatively authoritative edition but without the type of guide Ó Murchadha has now supplied. A 1993 reprint of Stokes' work by Dr Derek Bryce of Llanerch Publishers has again made the basic text more readily accessible. The monograph discussed here will greatly facilitate interaction with this indispensable document. Completing it has involved much more than mere mechanical listing. Judicious cross-referencing to related information within Tigernach augments the profile of many individual entries in the separate indexes. Parallel data from other annals are often drawn upon to supplement notices in the main source. Notes to both Irish personal names and particularly place-name entries reflect Ó Murchadha's expertise in family and tribal history, and give a glimpse of his current extensive researches into Ireland's onomastic traditions.

Unlike the Irish dimension to his work, the writer does not include precise identification of Roman emperors or locations mentioned in Scripture, for instance. This may be in the belief that such information is widely known. Mention of the guidelines laid out when the indexer consulted with authorities in the field of classical studies concerning non-Irish data, or of certain standard *Hilfsmittel* in this field, might have been useful here. Nevertheless, creating separate overseas indexes is greatly to the compiler's credit insofar as it draws attention to this country's awareness of and dealings with the outside world during medieval times. As we have seen, these issues figure under other guises elsewhere within the Subsidiary Series and the Society's main publications. Ó Murchadha's volume differs somewhat from its predecessors in both nature and scope. However, it adheres admirably to the Irish Texts Society's general ambition by concentrating on a specific compilation in order to reveal this composition's many treasures.

The Subsidiary Series just considered and the main editions they seek to supplement thus represent a most valuable and innovative contribution to both Gaelic scholarship and the wider sphere of Irish studies. They make available a diverse range of primary sources for key elements of this island's culture, and furnish informed critical opinion relating to their composition, purpose and intent. All those interested in Ireland's past will join in wishing the Irish Texts Society the same success in time to come as it has demonstrably achieved during its first century of operations, whether in providing fresh new material or causing us to recall once more the richness of what it has already brought to light.

CHAPTER FOUR

Connections, Friendships, and Concerns: Some Reminiscences

D. Ellis Evans

It was my privilege to be the President of the Irish Texts Society for nearly a decade and a member of its Council for considerably longer. Belonging to this Society as a member and officer was an enlightening and very joyous experience. I declare at once that its greatest joy for me was that it brought me into contact with a remarkable mix of people committed to serving the Society in various ways, administrative, cultural, scholarly, critical and, most importantly, truly caring. Welsh and Oxford connections with this Society go back to the very beginning in the person of F. York Powell, Regius Professor of Modern History in the University of Oxford, the first Chairman of its Executive Committee (not without a turbulent advent to the Chair - he did, we are told, regard himself as Welsh, although our perception of that must now alas be very limited, despite all that was written about him). I succeeded Professor Idris L. Foster as President. He was the third Jesus Professor of Celtic at Oxford from 1947 to 1978 and my distinguished predecessor in that unique Oxford Chair.

It is proper to refer briefly at the outset to some of my earlier connections with Ireland. These came first of all through the teaching I had as a young undergraduate in the University of Wales at both Aberystwyth and Swansea. At Aberystwyth the illustrious Professor T. H. Parry Williams, who had been taught by Edward Anwyl, John Rhys, Rudolf Thurneysen and Joseph Vendryes, brought to life an awareness of some of the importance of the Irish language in his quite lively teaching of historical and comparative Celtic philology. By the time I was taught by him he had, not surprisingly, as I now perceive it, become disillusioned by the excesses of Neo-Grammarian proclivities - he was most renowned in his own lifetime as a poet, essayist, and critic of great distinction.

At Swansea, to which I could migrate within the University of Wales, following the untimely death of my father, I was taught in the

Department of Classics by two altogether remarkable Irishmen. The one was the cultured and learned Head of Classics, Professor Benjamin Farrington, a gentle person who had no time for fools – an exceptionably able man of Cork origin with a hauntingly mellifluous Cork accent – his brother was Assistant Secretary of the Royal Irish Academy. He was for a long time an active Marxist, following a period of university teaching in South Africa at Witwatersrand University, and I remember him fondly as a most inspiring teacher of so much relating to Classical Greek civilisation, especially Greek Philosophy (he wrote mostly on what he rightly preferred to term Greek Science). The other was Willie Smith, a graduate of Trinity College, Dublin, who was a distinguished and sensitive expert on Latin elegeiac poetry *inter alia*, especially the memorably sensitive quality of the work of Propertius and the exceedingly complex manuscript tradition of his work. He was a contemporary of David Greene at Trinity College and an affectionately remembered eccentric bachelor – he had many obsessive interests, including a most touching and sensitive concern about countless details relating to Dublin buses (his obsession could vary, but Dublin was always, I think, uppermost). The unforgettable accents and special tones and great learning of these two kindly scholars enriched, jointly, my best early teaching in Classical Greek and Latin. Their guidance loomed large in my undergraduate studies in both Honours Latin and Honours Greek classes at Swansea. In July 1952, after completing study for my initial degree, my altogether determined Welsh Professor at Swansea, Henry Lewis, a Celtic philologist of international renown, rightly insisted that I should attend the new and promising Summer School pioneeringly arranged by the School of Celtic Studies of the Dublin Institute for Advanced Studies when it was at its early best, with a strong and renowned cutting edge. This was particularly enriching. I met there a number of Ireland's most distinguished scholars and a truly remarkable international gathering of young scholars of my generation, many of whom were later destined to become decidedly prominent in Irish and Celtic circles. This memorable experience was followed by an all too short but especially memorable visit to the West Kerry Gaeltacht, greatly encouraged by the inspiring and caring Father Tadhg Ó Murchú of Cork. I stayed at Dunquin and indeed visited the Great Blasket just before the old inhabitants had left. Later that 1952 summer I met Peig Sayers as well on the mainland when she was ailing in hospital. It was that summer too that I first saw for myself the amazing wonders of Newgrange.

I have mentioned these matters because they were, I am certain, especially important for my becoming more fully conscious as years went by of the paramount importance of Ireland and its history and culture (not least its Celtic language and rich native literature) for the study of so much connected with Celtic Studies which soon came to loom ever larger in my life as a University teacher at both Swansea and Oxford.

A competent assessment of the achievements of the Irish Texts Society is not easily determined and described in a celebratory volume which is designed to reflect among other things some of the quality of its publications and other activities. My limited purpose is to try to convey something of its special character and true quality as perceived by me over the last twenty years or so, a period during which, as I know, every effort was made to further the declared aims of the Society and to secure the continuation of its activities into the future according to the best tradition maintained by earlier generations of scholars. It is this commitment, camaraderie, and concern that has sustained and impressed so many who have been associated with the work of the Society. Insofar as I can sense and perceive the history and development of the Society the same could be said of it from the very outset.

The Society's consistently declared and carefully maintained purpose has been 'to advance public education by promoting the study of Irish literature, and as ancillary thereto to publish texts in the Irish language, accompanied by such introductions, English translations, glossaries and notes as may be deemed desirable'. My knowledge of its minute books, some of its papers, and especially its published volumes and my direct involvement in many of its activities in recent years convinces me that it has respected its 'objects', as they are usually termed, with very considerable devotion. The publication of fifty nine volumes along with Dinneen's mighty Dictionary, as well as the effort to keep as many volumes as possible in print and, in recent years, to develop a valuable and attractive subsidiary series of publications are clear evidence of its commitment to honour its central purpose.

The preparation of high quality editorial work requires so much painstaking involvement with detailed critical analysis of many aspects of the text presented. Despite some well-known inadequacies in a number of its publications, the Society's record in seeking to maintain high standards has overall been a good one. Very many of Ireland's foremost scholars have been involved in its publications. Success in maintaining high standards in the publications of the Society, as I know from my own involvement as one of its officers, calls for a dogged persistence and a special brand of quiet resilience and dynamism. It is not all that easy to seek out new editors, to coax and encourage them, to obtain unbiased and constructive advice from referees and especially to face up to the duty of firmly and politely excluding unsatisfactory work.

It is proper to stress that the Society has endeavoured to further its aims by arranging functions, social events and gatherings other than business meetings, to draw attention to matters relating to its publications and to subjects connected with the study of Irish literature. Most of these have taken place in recent years at the Irish Club in London's Eaton Square, a venue that is both homely and lingeringly grand. However, there have been fairly regular meetings in Ireland as well, especially of late. I refer to some of these events, in no special order or ranking. I recall clearly a well-attended meeting to celebrate the publication of a reprint of the four volumes of Geoffrey Keating's *Foras Feasa ar Éirinn,* including a deluxe version, with a new Introduction by Professor Breandán Ó Buachalla, who addressed the meeting which was held in the Bank Centre in Ballsbridge in Dublin in July 1986. Professor Máire Herbert addressed a meeting in London in April 1989 to mark the publication of *Betha Adamnáin,* edited by herself in collaboration with Professor Pádraig Ó Riain. Professor Ó Riain in June 1995, by then the Society's President, lectured to a large audience at the Irish Club to mark the publication of his edition of *Beatha Bharra* (*St Finbarr of Cork: the Complete Life*), and of a volume of the flourishing Subsidiary Publications Series to which Professors Joep Leerssen, J. Falaky Nagy and Erich Poppe and Drs John Carey and Diarmuid Ó Murchadha have recently contributed.

A reception was held in Dublin in October 1993 to mark the publication of Dr Caoimhín Mac Giolla Léith's edition of *Oidheadh Chloinne hUisneach* and Dr Carey's new introduction to *Lebor Gabála Érenn.* Professor Ó Riain also addressed the Society in June 1996 in London to celebrate the publication of another reprint, in a new format, of Patrick Dinneen's *Irish-English Dictionary*, a work still commanding great respect and continuing to be the Society's best seller. There was also a special Dublin launch of this reprint to coincide with the autumn 1996 meeting of the Society's Council. In this context I want to recall especially the delivery of the late Noel O'Connell's lecture to an invited audience at the Irish Club in September 1984 to mark the fiftieth anniversary of Dinneen's death. Noel, the Society's devoted Secretary, relished delivering that sensitive and discerning lecture to a large audience on 'Father Dinneen: his Dictionary and the Gaelic Revival'. It was published as a *separatum* by the Society. It is worthy of note once again, for sure, in this celebratory volume that Dinneen himself in his Preface to his new, revised and greatly enlarged Dictionary published in 1927 had said of the Irish Texts Society: 'I sometimes think of that Society as a distinctive university unchartered and unendowed, in which, though unworthy, I have been filling a "Chair" since the year 1900 when they published my *editio princeps* of O'Rahilly, in which I had kind assistance from Prof. Bergin'. It was after the delivery of that lecture that Noel O'Connell rightly decided that a Council meeting of the Irish Texts Society should not be called to order until a copy of Dinneen's fine Dictionary was resting on the table.

Members of the Irish Literary Society have been faithful attenders of 'open' meetings announced by the Irish Texts Society. Occasionally meetings would be arranged jointly by both Societies. This was appropriate for several obvious reasons, not least because the Texts Society was in its origin an offspring of the Literary Society and in recent years they both met in the Irish Club in Eaton Square. One instance of such a joint meeting occurred in March 1990 at which Professor Seán Ó Tuama, from University College, Cork, delivered a lecture on 'Aogán Ó Rathaille – greatest Irish poet before Yeats?'. Egan O'Rahilly's poems were edited for the Society in its early days by Dinneen (*Dánta Aodhagáin Uí Rathaille*, vol. 3, 1900, replaced by a new edition by Tadhg Ó Donnchadha and Dinneen, vol. 3a, 1911).

Another memorable meeting of the Society was addressed by the then President, Professor Idris Foster, in Cork in September 1982. The meeting was held at Jury's Hotel and, in accordance with the Society's welcoming custom, was preceded by a reception. He took as his subject ''The Irish Texts Society, 1898-1982: Retrospect and Prospect'. Professor Foster had been digging deep into the minute books and his own rich personal fund of knowledge to regale his audience with many anecdotes. In May 1988, to celebrate the ninetieth anniversary of the founding of the Society, I addressed an open meeting of the Society in London on 'Edward Lhuyd and Celtic Studies', drawing attention on the one hand to Lhuyd's great distinction as a polymath, especially as the founder of comparative Celtic philology and collector of so very many important manuscripts, many of which have been preserved as primary sources of vital importance for the study of a wide range of Irish literature, and on the other hand to the need to safeguard and redouble our efforts to make proper and better provision for the internationally respected discipline of Celtic Studies in our Universities, especially in Britain and Ireland.

By and large, attendance at meetings of committees, councils and all manner of boards can be exceedingly boring and wearisome - I know that I have attended considerably more than my fair share of such gatherings. However, I can say without any hesitation whatsoever that being present at Council meetings of the Irish Texts Society was always rewarding and agreeable. I say that in all honesty and I hope that potential or budding new members of Council will heed my remarks! Meetings of the Society's Council in London have been held regularly at the Irish Club. In the last twenty years I can think of only one exception in London when there was a Council and Annual General Meeting (most surprisingly, but very pleasantly) in the vicinity of Westminster Cathedral in March 1992. On that occasion one of the happiest and well considered events for the Society was the election of Professor Pádraig Ó Riain as President, proposed from the Chair by myself. This was all the more important a change because it came fairly soon after the death of our Secretary Noel O'Connell.

In all Council meetings business would be conducted carefully and efficiently. However, it would be fair to add that we rarely moved at anything approaching a brisk pace even after a tardy start following enjoyable gossiping well after the time announced for the meetings. The agenda would invariably concentrate on minutes, reports on business transacted between meetings and on financial statements, consideration of stocks of published volumes, reprints, readers' reports, new volumes, the pricing and supply and distribution of volumes, elections, correspondence, audits and various other management matters arising – all relating to the vital core purpose of the Society. This business would be conducted patiently and, in my experience of it, with no unpleasant disagreements or arguments. It is as though the unwavering commitment to seek to work together to serve the Society as effectively as possible kept bickering and backbiting altogether at bay. There were, for sure, occasional differences of opinion and conflicting and critical advice would sometimes reach us from unexpected quarters.

What I really want to dwell on a little more here, however, centres on what my experience and perception reveal to be the secret of the success of this Society. Firstly, I am certain that above all else the membership of its Council all the while was a decisive factor, a membership maybe unconsciously developed to be a remarkable blend of people from quite a considerable variety of walks of life. This resulted in a coming together of not only a good range of dedicated teachers from schools and universities but also of experienced people from various other professions such as banking, the civil service, engineering and telecommunications. Care was also taken to draw in a proper mix of people from both Ireland and Britain, especially well motivated members from London where the Society had its first inspiration and crucial support a hundred years ago and where it has retained its old and true centre. I very much hope that it will long retain its respect for that sustaining base and foundation. Secondly, the Society has been singularly fortunate in its officers throughout its history. I am sure that careful reference will have been made to this elsewhere in the present volume. My direct experience is of course limited to the period of my own close connection with the Society. It is right and proper to mention in particular that we have had great good fortune in having had a remarkable combination of gifted holders of the key offices of Honorary Secretary, Honorary Treasurer and, latterly, Honorary General Editor.

As a Past President I can, I hope, stand back dispassionately and pay tribute to the devotion of so many people who have served the Society with great care and commitment for long periods. The Society's papers and minute books do reflect a great deal of their involvement and contribution. However, personal knowledge of the individuals concerned and knowing at first hand more than a little of their work for the Society and so much of what it represented did over the years help to enrich one's perception and appreciation of the special attributes and commitment of many individuals.

It is appropriate, I think, that I should draw attention here to a small number of examples of devoted individuals as representatives of the great host of people who have served the Society in so many ways. To select names is exceedingly difficult and I do so with great diffidence. I decided, after much pondering, to refer only to the three members of the Society's Council who passed away during my period in office as President.

Idris Foster, who died in 1984, was the Society's President from

1973 to 1983. Before that he had been Treasurer from 1967 to 1972. During his Presidency he showed a special concern for maintaining high standards of scholarship in works published by the Society and for the establishing of new and efficient methods of distribution of the Society's publications. He also recognised the importance of securing charitable status for the Society. He was a modest, self-effacing and most learned Celtic scholar. A native of Bethesda in Caernarfonshire, he became Head of the Department of Celtic in the University of Liverpool and thereafter was Jesus Professor of Celtic in the University of Oxford. He won high acclaim in Oxford both as an enthusiastic teacher and as a patient and thoughtful supervisor of the research work of his numerous postgraduate students. His distinction as a scholar was matched by his outstanding service to many institutions, especially in Wales, Oxford itself, and London. Beyond all else he was a devoted Welshman. He took on the Presidency of the Irish Texts Society after the sudden death of his distinguished predecessor, the late Professor Myles Dillon. Professor Foster was a most kindly person, a man of great fortitude and integrity who worked quietly and efficiently for a long time for the furtherance of the declared aims of the Society.

Seán Barry, who died in 1989, was a Cork City man who had spent his working life in Britain. When I came to know him he lived in Worthing in Sussex and worked as an Inspector of Taxes for the Department of Inland Revenue. He was a most loyal and conscientious member of Council who fully realised the special role the Society had to play and the importance of sustaining it in accordance with its best traditions. He, I should stress, had a particular regard and respect for the Society's origins in London and the importance of firmly resisting all tendencies to sever the London links. He discreetly voiced his great concern that there might be increasing pressure to transfer most or all of the activities of the Society to Ireland. His advice always commanded great respect in Council meetings – he was ever watchful that we should take the right decisions, especially when it came to matters connected with finance and with proffering advice to editors, advice which he insisted should be clear, fair and firm, not least when we had to reject some unsatisfactory proposals put to us. He loved to talk about the Cork of his youth and his periodic visits there. He and Noel O'Connell were very close friends. They shared a great interest in the Irish language and all other things Irish and had helped each other a lot in many ways. That kind of friendship greatly helped to sustain the

Society, especially when lack of progress with the preparation and publishing of texts was worrying or when some, usually relatively minor, problems were a distraction.

Noel O'Connell's sudden death in May 1991 was a grievous loss for the Society, although I have most happy memories of the way several members of Council rallied round immediately to press on with the work in hand, collaborating harmoniously to plan the way ahead, with bright new faces very soon coming to cheer us and to give a new lead in shouldering responsibilities. Noel had moved to London in 1950 following graduation in Engineering at University College, Cork, and a year's teaching as a Junior Lecturer in that College. The *Irish Times* 'appreciation' of his life declared that 'He emerged [from his native Cork] with an engineering degree, fluency in the Irish language and a mind richly stocked with his country's literature, history and culture. Allied with these were a scholarly disposition, a strong sense of justice, a sharp wit and a talent for communication ... Noel was a rare combination of technical expert, scholar, teacher, humanitarian and family man'. Apart from a brief return to Dublin to work for the Electricity Supply Board in 1955 he followed his career thereafter in London as a consultant civil engineer, combined increasingly in later years with the teaching of engineering at South Bank Polytechnic, Thames Polytechnic and North East Surrey College of Technology. He also contributed a great deal to the development of Irish Studies at Kilburn Polytechnic. He was Chairman of the Greater London Council's Brent London-Irish Commission for Education and Culture and of London's Irish Club in Eaton Square. He helped to establish the Camden Irish Centre and the Threshold Housing Association. He joined the Irish Texts Society in 1958 and very soon became a Council member. He became Honorary Treasurer in 1962 and Honorary Secretary in 1967. When he died in 1991 he was 61 years of age (he had made a remarkable recovery from a stroke he had suffered eleven years earlier). My own tribute to his memory on behalf of the Society was published in 1991 as a preamble to Volume 55 of the series of texts published by the Society, namely *Stair Nicoméid* edited by Dr Ian Hughes. Writing this essay six years later brings back to me so many vivid memories of his rare qualities, not least his friendship, great kindness and gentleness, contagious enthusiasm and discerning and penetrating sense of humour. He managed the affairs of the Society with patience and devotion. This, it should be remembered, was only one of several indications of his loyalty to the language and culture of the Ireland he knew well and loved so much and his honest concern for the welfare of Irish people in London. I fear that people of his calibre are too often asked to do far too much. Noel O'Connell, as another member of the Council of the Texts Society declared when he realised our loss, can justifiably be remembered and portrayed as a great yet simple and humble man – a very special tribute and expression of respect, knowing as I do the person who shared his innermost thoughts with me. Another Irish friend at Oxford, one who has devoted so much of his time to the earnest and concerned teaching of Irish, described Noel in a letter to me as 'a gentle knowledgeable man who laboured diligently in the cause of the language he loved, and a credit to his country'. He was certainly that and much more.

Such are the kind of people who have served and still serve the Irish Texts Society. As we near the celebration of the centenary of the Society's foundation I know very well that its capable officers and other Council members still value greatly their connection with it and continue to serve it in a peculiarly unselfish way, with so much enthusiasm. The officers of the Society perform their duties with great professional efficiency and dedication. In all my experience over the years both Council meetings and 'open' meetings have invariably been truly joyous occasions, bringing together a relatively small, but warm-hearted and concerned band of people with common interests and common bonds and loyalties uniting them all the while. Many, many times have eating tables in the Irish Club in London or in its vicinity been the scene for the friendly and not infrequently critical discussion or chatter of members of the Society, talking in an altogether leisurely way on all manner of topics, including the mock rivalry of Cork and Kerry people, the colour of Irish postboxes,the peculiar ways of priests, poets, and politicians, sporting prowess, the Irish and Welsh rugby teams' hopes and failures, the nastiness of London's murky underworld (especially that of the Metropolitan Police), the state of the Irish Club, the frailties of academics and the misfortune of not belonging to one of the 'Celtic' peoples (that was a common and ever important deep baseline!). Long may that special joy continue and long may the work of the Irish Texts Society continue to be managed caringly with the unselfish and remarkable commitment, enthusiasm and tact which so many individuals have brought to its worthy activities now for a full century.

ARCHIVES AND DOCUMENTS

CHAPTER FIVE

Council of Society and its Officers

Pádraig Ó Riain

Initial Membership

As initially constituted, Council consisted of the following members: President, Douglas Hyde; Joint Hon. Secretaries, Norma Borthwick, Eleanor Hull; Hon. Treasurer, R. A. S. Macalister; Chairman of Council, F. York Powell; Vice-Chairman, Goddard H. Orpen; Members, A. Nutt,[89] T. J. Flannery,[90] J. G. O'Keeffe, D. Mescal, G. A. Greene, Michael O'Sullivan. Norma Borthwick seems to have left London for Dublin about this time and accordingly was given responsibility only for business relating to Ireland; her name figures rarely in the minutes.[91] R. A. S. Macalister relinquished the treasurership before the end of the year, on 12.10.1898.

Presidents

For its first sixty years the office of President of the Society was almost purely honorary. The first President, Douglas Hyde, at most attended two or three meetings during his very long tenure from 1898 until his death in 1949. After a short interval the position was then accepted by T. F. O'Rahilly.[92] After his death in 1953, however, the office remained vacant for two years, until Gerard Murphy, who had

---

89 Nutt had written a letter to the *Daily Chronicle* offering to 'publish as much as any Gael can desire. If 250 Irishmen will engage to subscribe 10s. 6d. a year for ten years'. His letter was reprinted in *Irisleabhar na Gaedhilge* 88 (August, 1897). His firm was the Society's publisher until 1916. See also pp. 16-18 above.

90 Flannery (1846-1916), better known under the Irish form of his name as Tomás Ó Flannghaile, appears to have had a leading role in the events that led to the foundation of the Society (Breathnach, Ní Mhurchú, *1882-1982: Beathaisnéis a hAon,* 71-2).

91 For an account of this remarkably talented woman, who was taught Irish by T. J. Flannery, see Breathnach, Ní Mhurchú, *1882-1982: Beathaisnéis a Dó,* 21-4.

92 For a note of O'Rahilly's letter of acceptance, see below at p. 103.

often acted on behalf of the Society in Dublin, became President. He was succeeded in 1959 by Myles Dillon, the first holder of the office to preside regularly over meetings of Council and to involve himself in decision-making. Dillon held the position until his death in 1972 and was succeeded in the following year by Idris Foster, the first occupant of a Chair at Oxford, and the first Welshman, to become a member of Council since F. York Powell was elected in 1898.[93] In the year before his death in 1984, after ten years service, Foster retired from the Presidency to which his fellow-countryman and successor in the Chair of Celtic at Jesus College, Oxford, D. Ellis Evans, was then elected. Professor Evans also served as President for ten years, until 1992, when he was succeeded by the present holder of the office, Professor Pádraig Ó Riain of University College, Cork.[94]

Vice-Presidents

Even more symbolic and honorary in its role was the Vice-Presidency of the Society. From an original composition of no fewer than eight in 1898 the office gradually declined in size to one lone survivor in 1934, Lord Castletown. In 1935 Tomás Ó Deirg, Minister for Education in the Irish Government was elected Vice-President, to be joined in 1938 by Archbishop Michael Sheehan. Ó Deirg was subsequently also joined by Risteárd Ó Maolchatha, Minister for Education in the first Coalition Government, in 1949 before the office was finally allowed to lapse.

Chairmen

In the sixty years preceding M. Dillon's Presidency Council meetings were presided over by elected Chairmen or their representatives. The first Chairman was a Welshman, Frederick York Powell (1898-1901), Professor of History at Oxford and an 'ardent champion of Irish learning'.[95] York Powell's election at the Inaugural General Meeting,

93 R. Bromwich, the noted Welsh scholar, was elected to Council a little later than Foster in 1967.

94 D. Ellis Evans provides a valuable personal review of his association with the Society in this volume at pp. 57-66.

95 He is so described by his friend Kuno Meyer in the dedication to the latter's edition of *Cáin Adamnáin* (Oxford, 1905).

which was initially chaired by R. Barry O'Brien representing the Irish Literary Society, marked the emergence of the Irish Texts Society in its own right.[96] After Powell this position of responsibility was occupied successively by D. Mescal (1902-05), J. Buckley (1906-11), T. A. England (1912), F. MacDonagh (1913), and T. W. Rolleston (1914).[97] The first scholar of Irish to be elected to the chair was Robin Flower who held the office for over thirty years, from 1915 until a few months before his death in 1946. Flower's successor, longtime friend and fellow scholar, A. Martin Freeman,[98] retained the position until his death in 1959 at which point, owing to the introduction of a more active Presidency by M. Dillon, the Chairmanship of Council became obsolete. A Vice-Chairmanship, instituted in 1898 and occupied successively by G. H. Orpen and D. Mescal, was discontinued in 1901.

Hon. Secretaries

The Society has been particularly fortunate in its choice of incumbents of this critically important office. The length of service of its Hon. Secretaries to date is in itself a measure of their devotion to the Society. Beginning with E. Hull (1897-1918),[99] successive Hon. Secretaries have been T. D. Fitzgerald (1918-28), Maurice O'Connell (1928-65), who shared with Eleanor Hull the distinction of being the longest serving active officer of the Society,[100] and Noel O'Connell (1967-91),[101] following whose untimely death the office passed to

96 I wish to thank Pádraigín Riggs for pointing out to me the symbolic character of the alternation in the chairmanship at this meeting.

97 See Breathnach, Ní Mhurchú, *1882-1982: Beathaisnéis a hAon,* 110-1.

98 For Freeman (1878-1959), see ibid., 39-40.

99 For an account of this outstanding and many-sided scholar, who used as the Irish form of her name Eibhlín Nic Choill, see ibid., 33-4. She remained on as Joint Hon. Secretary with Fitzgerald until 1928, when she again became full Hon. Secretary in name until her death in 1935. (The minutes were actually kept from 1928 on by Maurice O'Connell who was first called Assistant Secretary.)

100 His term of office was exceeded only by Douglas Hyde who was President from 1898 until his death in 1949. Hyde's post was, however, purely honorary. For an account of O'Connell, see the 'London Letter' of *The Cork Examiner* 20 April, 1968.

101 See D. Ellis Evans, 'In Memoriam Noel O'Connell 1929-1991', in I. Hughes, ed. *Stair Nicoméid* (Irish Texts Society 55, 1991) i-iv.

David Sexton who acted as Hon. Secretary until Seán Hutton was elected to the the post in 1992. A post of Assistant Secretary, which apparently did not involve membership of Council, was filled successively between 1901 and 1912 by Miss Dodd (1901-2), Miss M. MacMahon (1903-6) and Mr. J. Campbell (1907-12). In the 1920s T. D. Fitzgerald's wife acted as his Assistant.[102]

Hon. Treasurers

Beginning with R. A. Macalister in 1898, the holders of this very important and demanding office have been J. G. O'Keeffe (1899), T. B. MacDowell (1900), P. J. Boland (1901-2), M. Dodd (1903), D. Mescal (1904-5), S. Boyle (1906-20), T. A. England (1921-30), and M. C. Lynch (1931-56), who has been the longest serving treasurer to date. Lynch was followed by K. Coady (1956-62), N. O'Connell (1962-7), I. Foster (1967-72), R. Bromwich (1972-7), and G. A. O'Mahony (1977-1981). Since 1981 the post has been held by Michael J. Burns.

Hon. Auditors

The Society's first auditors were Frank MacDonagh, later also a member of Council, and Mr. J. D. Noonan. Various auditors followed, including for 1912 T. D. Fitzgerald (Tomás D. MacGearailt) who was later to become Hon. Secretary. Then for more than thirty years, 1921-1958, the accounts of the Society were audited by Robert W. Farrell. With his successor, Brian Magee (1958-74), the title of Hon. Auditor began to be used. Magee was followed by G. A. O'Mahony (1975-7), who is still a member of Council, and the present Hon. Auditor, Dónal MacSweeney, formerly also a member of Council, who has now given twenty-one years of service.

Hon. Editors

Since 1977 Council has nominated a member with special responsibility for publications. Rachel Bromwich was first designated Secretary for Publications, her title being changed to that of Hon.

102 See also p. 84 below.

General Editor in 1983. Dr Bromwich retired from the office in 1984 and her successor, the present holder, was Brendan Bradshaw. The previous practice of seeking advice from scholars from within and without Council when choosing editors of volumes and when seeking guidance on the quality of work presented has, however, continued in place.

Consultative Committee

At the Inaugural General Meeting of the Society several scholars of national and international standing, including Henri Gaidoz, P. W. Joyce, Eoin Mac Neill, Kuno Meyer, Holger Pedersen, and Rudolf Thurneysen, were nominated to membership of a Consultative Committee. Changes in membership were occasionally minuted as the Commitee remained in place for seventy years, until 30.3.1968, when a decision was taken to discontinue it.

American Committee

An American Committee of the Society was set up in 1912 on the initiative of the Arthurian scholar, A. C. L. Brown. Included among its members were the heads of Notre Dame University and Catholic University, Washington, as well as John Quinn, a well-known New York lawyer and supporter of the cause of Ireland,[103] and three established American Celtic scholars of the time, Tom Peete Cross, Joseph Dunn and F. N. Robinson.[104]

Venues of Meetings

For more than forty years Council of the Society has been meeting at the Irish Club, Eaton Square, London. This was the culmination of a long odyssey around West Central London, mainly in response to various changes of address of the parent Irish Literary Society. The Inaugural General Meeting, for example, was held 'in the Rooms of the Irish Literary Society' at 8 Adelphi Terrace, Strand, London, W.C.

103 Cf. B. L. Reid, *The Man from New York: John Quinn and his Friends* (New York, 1968).

104 For the full list of members, see *Annual Report* [1912] 5.

Among subsequent venues of meetings were 57 Long Acre (1902), 20 Hanover Square (1904-19), with some use in between of such venues as 'The Writers Club', Norfolk St., Strand, (5.10.1909), and 16 John's St., Adelphi, (15.5.1914-25.11.1915). The new address of 7, Brunswick Square, W.C.I, (1920) was vacated in January 1922, after which such addresses as 9 Brunswick Square, Windsor House, Victoria St., 28 John St. and the N.U.I. Club, 13 Grosvenor Square, are noted in the minutes before the decision on 22.1.1955 to make what proved to be the final move to the Irish Club in Eaton Square.

Mailing Address

For the first twenty or so years the Society's mailing address for communication with members changed in accordance with its own changes of address. In 1922, however, an arrangement was made with National Bank Ltd., Charing Cross, London, to have it act as the Society's covering address and, subject to switches of branches (Whitehall from 1931), this situation remained unaltered until the 1980s when The Royal Bank of Scotland, first of Whitehall, later of Charing Cross, replaced it. Since 1996 communications can also be sent directly to the Hon. Secretary or Hon. Treasurer.

Annual Reports

Reports of 52 Annual General Meetings of the Society were printed for distribution to members, but this practice was discontinued in 1950. Many of the early volumes published by the Society contain copies of these reports as appendices.

Publishers, Printers and Binders

Volumes 1-16 were published and distributed by David Nutt of London whose proprietor, Alfred Nutt, was a member of the first Executive Council. These volumes were in the main printed at the University Press, Dublin. The Society itself seems to have looked after Volume 17 which was printed by Dundalgan Press, Dundalk. The publisher and distributor of Volumes 18-32 was Simpkin, Marshall, Kent and Co., London, who availed of the services of various printers. M. H. Gill and Son, Dublin, which published, with the Gaelic League, Dinneen's 1904 Dictionary, and The Educational Company of Ireland,

Dublin, which published and distributed Dinneen's 1927 Dictionary, as well as Volumes 29a, 33-48, were the first Irish firms to act for the Society. The Educational Company included among its staff An Seabhac who took a great interest in the Society's affairs, and later Kevin Etchingham who continues to consult with printers on behalf of the Society. With Volume 49 the Society began to act as its own publisher and acted as distributor also until ÁIS was established in 1978. Various printers have been employed. The last three volumes, and all the publications in the Subsidiary Series, were printed by Elo Press, Dublin. Among binders of volumes have been Galwey and Co., Dublin, Brindley and Co., Dublin, John English, Wexford, and Duffy Binders, Dublin.

Present Council

The present Council is composed of the following members, with year of election added in brackets: President, Pádraig Ó Riain (1976); Hon. Secretary, Seán Hutton (1989); Hon. Treasurer, Michael J. Burns (1981); Hon. Editor, Brendan Bradshaw (1979); Members, D. Ellis Evans (former President, 1978), Máire Herbert (1995), Máire Ní Mhaonaigh (1997), Breandán Ó Buachalla (1988), Brian Ó Cuív (1984), G. A. O'Mahony (former Hon. Treasurer, 1975), and David Sexton (1986).[105] Bearnard Ó Dubhthaigh, who was elected in 1971, is Council's longest serving member.

105 Patrick Sims-Williams (1989) was a member of Council until his resignation in 1997. Pádraig Ó Conchúir (1970) had been a member of Council for twenty-seven years until his death in 1997.

CHAPTER SIX

Archives of the Society

Pádraig Ó Riain

Introduction

Minutes have been preserved of the meetings of the Society's Executive Council since 5.5.1898, when it first met, ten days after the Society's Inaugural General Meeting of 26.4.1898. Minutes have also been preserved of this latter meeting and of the eighteen preceding, preparatory meetings.[106] Fifteen of these concerned the Irish Texts Sub-Committee of the Irish Literary Society which first met on 24.5.1897;[107] three involved the Provisional Committee of the Irish Texts Society which, from 24.3.1898, made final preparations for the inauguration of the Society.

The minute books and other archival material were kept in the custody of successive Hon. Secretaries until after Noel O'Connell's death in 1991 when they passed to the acting Hon. Secretary, David Sexton. In late 1994 Council decided that the Society's Archives, excepting the more recent minute books and other materials, should be offered for safe keeping and greater ease of consultation to the Library of University College, Cork.[108] D. Sexton subsequently arranged for the documents to be transferred to Cork where they are now deposited.[109]

Included in the material now held in Cork are ten minute books, numbered 1, 3-11, ending with the minutes of the meeting held on 26.5.1987. Brief descriptions of the contents of these books are pub-

106 For the minutes of the Inaugural General Meeting and of the eighteen preparatory meetings that preceded it, see below pp. 104-22.

107 According to the first printed report of the Society, appended to Volume 1 of its published texts, a Provisional Subcommittee had already been set up in 1896, only to be disbanded because of the poor response to its appeal for support. See also pp. 9-12 above.

108 Consultation is permitted of all material relating to the the first seventy years of the Society's history, viz. 1898-1968.

109 One of the minute books (MB 11) initially went to M. J. Burns, who then arranged to have it transferred to Cork.

lished here. Minute book 2, which covers meetings between 21.1.1902 and 23.4.1907, was deposited in the National Library of Ireland, where it is numbered Manuscript G 567. By kind permission of the National Library a new account of its contents is given below.[110]

The miscellaneous other files of the Society now held in Cork, and briefly described below, mainly comprise correspondence of successive Hon. Secretaries with editors of volumes, members, publishers and printers. Some of this material is of considerable interest, most notably perhaps the correspondence relating to the publication of the enlarged Irish-English dictionary which was published in 1927. The numerous letters written by the editor, P. S. Dinneen, to the Society's Secretary, T. D. Fitzgerald, whose proud boast it was to have seen the Dictionary through the press, do not appear to have been available to the great lexicographer's biographers, P. Ó Conluain and D. Ó Céileachair, in 1958.[111] Also of interest, for the light it throws on the history of Irish textual scholarship since 1898, is the correspondence with editors of volumes and especially perhaps that relating to volumes promised but for various reasons never completed.

MINUTE BOOKS (ITS MB 1-11)

The minute books and other archival materials now held in the Library of University College, Cork, are in Box Files numbered 1-28; the ten minute books are in Boxes 1-5. In numbering the minute books 1-11, I have taken account of National Library Manuscript G 567 which is listed here as ITS MB 2.[112] In describing the minute books I have sought less to be comprehensive than to convey an idea of the matters that most preoccupied members of Council over the years.

Box 1 ITS MB 1 24.5.1897-3.12.1901

Paper copy book of 116 pages, bound in marbled boards, lacking spine. The minutes, which are kept throughout by Eleanor Hull, concern both the meetings of Executive Council and also those of the Committees that prepared the ground for the foundation of the

110 See also P. Ó Macháin, ed., *Catalogue of Irish Manuscripts in the National Library of Ireland* 11 (Dublin, 1990) 100-1.

111 P. Ó Conluain, D. Ó Céileachair, *An Duinníneach* (Dublin, 1958).

112 See note 110 above.

Society.[113] The minutes of the Inaugural General Meeting on 26.4.1898, which marked the finalization of the preparatory work preceding the founding of the Society, contain several lists of nominees to Committees. Also notable about these minutes is the attachment to them of two signatures of Chairmen, that of R. Barry O'Brien, representing the parent Irish Literary Society, who chaired the opening part of the meeting, and that of Frederick York Powell, representing the offspring Irish Texts Society, who was later installed in the chair.[114]

The urgent need of a good Irish-English dictionary to satisfy the demand created by the flourishing language movement had long been recognized and, at a meeting of the Provisional Committee on 21.4.1898, a letter was read from Fr Eugene O'Growney 'suggesting the advisability of a handy Irish dictionary'. Subsequently, on 1.7.1898, guidelines were drawn up for the production of such a dictionary and Fr Peter O'Leary (An tAthair Peadar) was invited to act as editor/supervisor. Later in the year, on 30.12, a Dictionary Sub-Committee was formed whose minutes, with one exception,[115] appear to have been lost. After more than a year of apparently little progress Fr O'Leary was succeeded on 6.2.1901 by John (Eoin) Mac Neill who also made little headway. He was replaced after a few months, on 17.7.1901, by David Comyn who was followed a week later by P. S. Dinneen. Fr Dinneen had earlier become involved in the work of the Society through his offer of an edition of the poems of Aodhagán Ó Rathaille (26.4.1899). There now began, however, an association which, although it was to prove, as Dinneen himself described it, 'a heavy burthen' both on himself and on the Society,[116] was to influence more than any other the reputation and financial well-being of both parties to it. The amount of space given over to the subject of the Dictionary in all minute books is quite considerable. In the course of his first letter on the subject Dinneen stated, as minuted (23.7.1901), that 'it would require a year's steady work, working four hours a day

113 See above at p. 21.

114 For another example of the attachment of two signatures, albeit on a less amicable basis, see below at p. 81.

115 For the lone surviving example, see below at p. 80.

116 P. S. Dinneen, *Foclóir Gaedhilge agus Béarla: an Irish-English Dictionary* (Dublin, 1927) xiii.

... to correct and amend the slips and see the dictionary through the press ... and that he could not undertake it for less that £250'. This concern with time and money, as well as with proper standards of editing, was to be a recurrent theme in Dinneen's correspondence with the Society.

The first volume to be published by the Society, *Giolla an Fhiugha: the Lad of the Ferule* (1899), was mentioned by name in the minutes of 3.3.1898 and again, with the editor and President of the Society, Douglas Hyde, in the chair, at the meeting of 6.7.1898. At the latter meeting mention was also made of a 'promised edition' of Keating's History of Ireland, presumably by D. Comyn who, a year previously, had published an edition of the Introduction or *Díonbhrollach* of the text.[117]

Evidence of some initial tensions in the deliberations of the Society is apparent in the minutes of 13.5.1898 which record a decision to write to and inform Mr. Laurence Ginnell that, in view of his letters to several members, Council did not think 'he could wish to retain his connection with a Society in the management of which he had no confidence'.[118]

NLI MS G 567 ITS MB 2 28.1.1902-2.4.1907

Copy book of 180 pages, bound in marbled boards with spine missing.[119] The hand throughout is that of Eleanor Hull. Many loose documents in numbered envelopes (i-xviii) are preserved inside the front cover. These consist mainly of communications relating to Society business received by Miss Hull from various scholars. Included are letters from J. MacErlean S. J. in connexion with a proposed edition of the Life of Colum Cille (5.9.1902), from O. J. Bergin, then in Cork, refusing to undertake an edition of the Contention of the Bards (18.4.1904),[120] and from Seaghán P.

117 D. Comyn, *Díonbhrollach Fórais Feasa ar Éirinn* (Dublin, 1898).

118 I have been unable to discover the cause of dissension.

119 For a previously published account of this minute book, see P. Ó Macháin, *Catalogue of Irish Manuscripts in the National Library of Ireland*, XI, (Dublin, 1990) 100-1. I am also grateful to P. Riggs for making available to me notes she copied from the manuscript.

120 This text was later edited for the Society by Lambert McKenna (Vols. 20-1, 1918).

MacÉnrí, then in Dublin, who, in tendering his resignation from Council, vigorously defended himself against an accusation that he had nearly involved the Society in a 'great misfortune' by recommending the young scholar 'Mr. O'Malley' (Tomás Ó Máille) as editor of Keating's History (15.1.1907). Ó Máille had been invited to complete the edition, abandoned by Comyn in a letter read to Council on 28.3.1905, only after many other scholars had been approached, including P. W. Joyce (28.3.1905), R. I. Best (7.11.1905) and M. E. Byrne (13.2.1906). The decision to employ him led to several letters to Council expressing dissatisfaction (8.5.1906). Miss Hull was finally authorised to write privately to Fr Dinneen in the hope that he would complete the work (28.11.1906). Fr Dinneen agreed but drove a hard financial bargain (19.12.1906, 8.1.1907).

During this whole period Dinneen's 1904 Dictionary was the main subject of discussion, the recurrent themes being the progress of the work and, most importantly for both Council and editor, money. Funds were sought and received from many sources, including the Irish bishops (5.1.1903). Generous loans were also made available by such benefactors as Albina Broderick, who gave £200, and J. P. Boland M. P., and J. Hill Twigg, who gave £100 each. Council proposed to print 2000 copies; Dinneen, showing far greater foresight, insisted on 5000. Within a few months of publication 1500 copies had been either ordered or sold and very soon the whole edition had been exhausted. Council offered prizes for lists of possible additions to a new edition, including interleaved copies of the Dictionary (loose insert xvi).

An edition of the Life of Colum Cille, which never materialised, engendered much correspondence (11.3.1902, 3.2.1903). An edition of the poems attributed to the same saint was suggested to Charles Plummer who felt he was not competent to undertake it (22.4.1902). Richard Foley (Risteard Ó Foghladha) made several proposals concerning editions of modern poetry (22.7.1902, 9.9.1902), none of which was proceeded with. J. H. Lloyd (Seosamh Laoide) was engaged in the preparation of an edition of the poem book of Aodh mac Sheáin Uí Bhroin (15.5.1906), later edited for the Dublin Institute for Advanced Studies by Seán Mac Airt.[121] Already by 13.5.1902, R. A. S. Macalister was in a position to send for approval part of his

121 S. Mac Airt, ed., *Leabhar Branach: The Book of the O'Byrnes* (Dublin, 1944).

edition of *Lebor Gabála Érenn*, which was not to begin to be published for another 36 years.[122] The progress of Eoin Mac Neill's edition of *Duanaire Finn* was followed with much anxiety because of its slowness (loose insert xvi). While still in the press its use was requested by Lady Gregory in a book she was working on (15.4.1903).

The possibility of the preparation of a 'Calendar of Irish manuscripts' was explored by Council in a circular issued in 1902. The response was disappointing. Robert Atkinson, who is best remembered not for his considerable contribution to Irish scholarship but for his negative testimony on the value of literature in Irish before the 1898 Commission of Enquiry into Intermediate Education, is reported to have declared that 'he would do Nothing'(written with capital) to assist the Society. An attempt to raise funds towards a catalogue of the manuscripts in the possession of the Royal Irish Academy was discussed on 11.9.1906. At its meeting of 21.5.1903 Council agreed to send a complete set of its publications to the German scholar Heinrich Zimmer who had lost his library through fire.

Box 1 ITS MB 3 28.5.1907-13.6.1912

Large copy book of 228 pages, bound in marbled boards with cloth spine. The hand throughout is that of Eleanor Hull. Loose inserts accompany various minutes, including the original of a letter from P. O'Kinealy, with an address at the East India United Service Club, London, minuted under 4.4.1912. The letter contains an offer to defray half the estimated cost of printing the fourth volume of Keating's History of Ireland which was published in 1914. O'Kinealy did not live to see the product of his generosity to the Society, which has never since been matched by a private individual.

Another loose insert of considerable interest between pp. 92-3 is the report of the Publications Sub-Committee of 12.6.1909, which represents the only surviving record of the deliberations of this group. As with the main minutes these also are in the hand of Eleanor Hull.

122 In the meantime he had published elsewhere with Eoin Mac Neill an edition of part of Mícheál Ó Cléirigh's recension of the same text (*Leabhar Gabhála. The Book of Conquests of Ireland. The Recension of Mícheál Ó Cléirigh,* Dublin, 1916), and it would seem that this was the recension he had first been editing for the Society (13.5.1904, 19.5.1905).

One of the main preoccupations of Council during this period was its increasing dissatisfaction with the Society's publisher and distributor, David Nutt. After sixteen volumes had been published by this firm, the Society's agreement with it was terminated on 23.5.1916. In the meantime, however, relations with the publisher had become a source of much discussion and occasional dissension. Disagreement on this subject, for example, led to the minutes for 24.11.1908, which had already been signed by W. Buckley, being partly crossed out whereupon, Mr. Buckley now refusing to resign them, they were countersigned by E. Collins.

The first edition of the Dictionary having been published in 1904, Fr Dinneen's name does not figure quite so prominently in the minutes of this period. His school dictionary, which was published in 1910, came up for discussion (3.8.1909), however, as did the possibility of a supplement to his 1904 publication (5.10.1909).

Among those preparing volumes for publication was T. F. O'Rahilly who, very much later, was elected President of the Society (1950). His offer of an edition of three Spanish Tales in Irish translation was first minuted on 3.8.1909 and, although never completed, this continued to be mentioned in minutes until 1938 when it was finally withdrawn.[123] (In 1935 it was handed over for completion to É. O'Toole (Éamonn Ó Tuathail), who soon tired of it and returned the work already done to O'Rahilly (12.2.1938).) During this period also a 'Supplementary Series' containing reprints of out of print Irish works of importance, such as the Annals of the Four Masters, was discussed but no action was taken (5.10.1909).[124]

Box 2 ITS MB 4 13.6.1912-17.12.1918

Large copybook of 246 pages, bound in marbled boards with a cloth spine. The minutes continue to be written by Eleanor Hull until 14.11.1918 when, due to pressure of other commitments, she was joined as Joint Hon. Secretary by T. D. Fitzgerald (Tomás D. Mac Gearailt).[125]

123 The tales in question, *novelas* by Juan Perez de Montalvan, which had been translated into Irish by Fr Manus Ó Domhnaill, are in Dublin, RIA MSS. 23 M 3, 23 M 10.

124 For another proposal of a Supplementary Series, see below at p. 86

125 See also note 99 above.

Fitzgerald had become a member of the Society in 1913 and had begun to attend meetings of Council on 29.11.1917. His first minutes of 17.12.1918 were typed.

The First World War impinged but little on the affairs of the Society. Among the matters reflecting it are an investment in War Loan stock (26.10.1915), a request from Ruhleben Camp for Irish books for use in classes (14.12.1916) and the nomination to the Consultative Committee of 'Prof. Capt. Vendryes' on 29.3.1917.

The Easter Rising of 1916 had a much more noticeable effect. Soon after it, on 23.5.1916, an Emergency Council meeting chaired by Robin Flower was told that 'Messrs Sealy and Bryers premises with their contents were entirely destroyed in the fires in Dublin during the recent riots', and a letter from P. S. Dinneen urged the Society to 'lose no time in instituting a claim for loss of the Society's Dictionary plates and property'. Dinneen suggested that a claim of about £750 be made and eventually the Society received £320 in compensation (14.12.1916).

The 1904 Dictionary having thus become a casualty of the Easter Rising, P. S. Dinneen promptly decided to prepare for publication a substantially larger and improved version.[126] This 'new enlarged Dictionary', which was eventually published in 1927, and which has since been reprinted several times, was discussed for the first time by Council on 31.5.1917, following the receipt of a letter from Fr Dinneen outlining his vision of the undertaking. He calculated that it would take four (instead of an eventual ten) years to complete, and proposed that he be remunerated at £100 per annum (subsequently (4.10.1917) emended to £160 'due to high cost of living') together with royalties of ten per cent. Council estimated that the total cost would be £1500 and, because it had then no more than £500 to invest, decided to raise a 'Guarantee Fund' (27.7.1917). A form of appeal for this fund, in Irish and English, was agreed on 14.2.1918 but the subsequent poor response from the public was attributed to 'changes in popular sentiment as regards the position of affairs in Ireland, as well as owing to the war' (9.5.1918).[127] The Dictionary and its Guarantee Fund were to account for more than their fair share of minutes over the next ten years.

126 Ó Conluain, Ó Céileachair, *An Duinníneach*, 233-4.

127 A copy of the Appeal is preserved in Dinneen File 1 (see below at p. 100).

During this period Council was of course also concerned with its other publications and one of these, Tomás Ó Máille's edition of Carolan's poems, now Volume 17, bears mentioning because of its uniqueness in the series. At its meeting of 29.6.1915 Council agreed to accept this volume for publication despite its lack of a translation of the poems into English. This proved to be the Society's only departure from its first General Rule which requires that all texts be 'accompanied by such Introductions, English Translations, Glossaries, and Notes, as may be deemed desirable'.

Box 2 ITS MB 5 1.2.1919-15.12.1924

Large copybook of 238 pages, bound in marbled boards with a cloth spine. There are several blank pages at the end (224-36) followed by a list of volumes in stock between 1920-24. The minutes, which are variously handwritten or typed, are by T. D. Fitzgerald. The executive Chairman, Robin Flower, chaired most meetings. Already, however, illness was delaying the completion of his volume of Medieval Translations, which he was to set aside altogether in 1925 (26.5.1924, 23.9.1924).

Dinneen's Dictionary figured prominently in the minutes, largely because of its slow progress, but also because it threatened to bankrupt the Society (28.1.1922). A grant of £1000 was offered by Dáil Éireann on condition that the Dictionary be sold at 7/6, which would have meant a considerable loss per volume to the Society. (Eventually, the grant was made but the price remained at the 12/6 fixed by the Society (2.7.1924).)[128] A contract was signed with the printers, Messrs Sealy, Bryers and Walker, on 11.10.1922.

Much space was also allocated in these minutes, especially during 1920-1, to the O'Neill Poems, then being edited for the Society by Tadhg O'Donoghue (Torna). The O'Neill of Lisbon had taken a particular interest in this volume which was making very slow progress.[129] The kernel of the problem was Torna's failure to satisfy Robin Flower's views on the translation of bardic verse and, after a long delay, his edition of the poems was published, without translation and

128 For a note on the correspondence relating to the grant, see below Dinneen File 2 (Box 15) at p. 100.

129 For the location of the correspondence, see below at p. 97.

without any recognition of the Society's role, by the Irish Manuscripts Commission.[130]

Delays in the Society's volumes were then, as ever, a source of great anxiety. The concern of Council is voiced in a minute of the meeting of 20.2.1924 which states that 'all our books were in arrears' and that 'in order to get up to date, it would be necessary to place in the hands of members no fewer than four volumes during 1924'. In fact, one volume only, C. O'Rahilly's edition of *Tóruigheacht Gruaidhe Griansholus*, was published in 1924, followed by a gap of five years, until 1929, when three volumes (25-7) appeared.

A survey of the Society's membership, which was minuted on 27.1.1923, showed the following pattern: 53% (Ireland), 23% (Great Britain), 17% (USA and Canada), with the remaining 7% presumably on the Continent. This broke down further into 62 members in Dublin, 52 in London, 103 in Leinster (outside Dublin), 101 in Munster, 37 in Connacht, and 34 in Ulster. Among new members from Connacht was An tAthair Mícheál Ó Gríobhtha of Galway (7.6.1920) regret at whose subsequent murder by English Crown Forces was also minuted (7.12.1920). Life membership was taken out by Domhnall Ua Corcora (Daniel Corkery) of Cork on 30.9.1920.

Box 3 ITS MB 6 31.1.1925-26.1.1929

A loose-leaved ring ledger of 230 pages, covered in black boards. The minutes were typed by T. D. Fitzgerald as far as 9.8.1928 when, having held the post of Joint Hon. Secretary for ten years, he resigned from it together with his wife who, although not a member of Council, had acted as his Assistant. Maurice O'Connell (Muiris Ó Conaill), who had already been suggested as Assistant Secretary on 15.7.1926, then took over the position.

130 T. Ó Donnchadha, eag., *Leabhar Cloinne Aodha Buidhe* (Baile Átha Cliath, 1931). In a letter to Torna dated 23.5.1922, which survived among the Cork scholar's papers and which is now in my possession, Flower wrote: 'There is much that I should like to discuss with you personally as to the shape of English to be adopted in the translation. I constantly feel that there is a danger of the bardic poets being misrepresented by a style of translation that keeps too close to the sense and idiom of the Irish. The Irish text is, no doubt, the main point. But so many of our Society are as yet incapable of reading this older Irish with any freedom, and a translation of both spirit and fidelity seems required to let them see the kind of thing the bards were aiming at'.

It was Fitzgerald's great achievement to have seen Dinneen's Dictionary successfully through the press. Despite enormous difficulties encountered along the way, many of which were created by the editor, the Dictionary was finally published late in the year 1927 and, at a Council meeting on 28.1.1928 one of two specially bound and interleaved copies of the work was proudly placed on the table by Fitzgerald.[131] Within a month of publication 2550 copies of the Dictionary had been sold.[132]

Robin Flower's volume on the Blasket Islands first came up for discussion on 10.11.1925, a full account of it being reserved for the minutes of 30.1.1926. A noticeable lack of enthusiasm for the proposal was displayed by some members of Council, probably because it meant that Flower would now give up entirely his work in progress on a volume of Medieval Translations.[133] In any case the proposal was adopted and, before the editor's failing health brought about the abandonment of the project in 1938,[134] approximately half of the volume, consisting largely of the Irish text of the tales, had been set up in type, which then had to be dispersed.[135]

Among those who joined the Society during this period were the prominent politicians Liam T. Mac Cosgair or W. T. Cosgrave (4.3.1927) and Seán T. Ó Ceallaigh (17.5.1928), and the writer Pádraic Colum (11.11.1927).

---

131 There is now no trace of this copy. The custom of having a copy of Dinneen's Dictionary on the table at meetings of Council was later revived by N. O'Connell.

132 Within two months, a note had been received by the Society warning it of an attack to be made on the work in *Gadelica* by Professors Bergin and O'Rahilly (16.2.1928). By then, however, *Gadelica* had long ceased to be published. Moreover, neither Bergin nor O'Rahilly reviewed the Dictionary.

133 The texts of the Medieval Translations included the Harrowing of Hell and other Apocryphal tales. An effort to have the edition taken up again under different editorship was made in 1934; see below at p. 99.

134 For mention of Flower's deteriorating health, see minutes 15.7.1926, 29.1.1927, 30.9.1932, 29.5.1933.

135 The volume was finally edited by S. Ó Duilearga for the Irish Folklore Commission as *Seanchas ón Oileán Tiar* (Dublin, 1956).

Box 3 ITS MB 7 12.3.1929-31.7.1943

A large ledger book of 244 pages, bound in half leather and marbled boards. Pasted inside the cover is a copy of the General Rules of the Society for 1934. A useful index of contents, compiled by the Secretary, Maurice O'Connell, also precedes the minutes proper.

Due, no doubt, to the success of the Dictionary, the Society was now well off financially, so much so that one of the few remaining founder members still active on Council, Eleanor Hull, found it necessary to encourage a reduction of the positive balance by proposing that editors' honoraria be increased from £40 to £50, that more rent be paid to the Irish Literary Society for the use of their rooms, and that future volumes be printed in Ireland (24.9.1931).

Dinneen's death was reported to Council at its meeting of 15.10.1934. No other editor influenced more the fortunes of the Society than he. Already by the end of 1933, 9500 copies of his Dictionary had been sold and by early 1934 Dinneen's views were being sought on the possibilitity of a Supplement (22.8.1934).[136] Even today, despite the pre-standard form of its letters and spelling, Dinneen's Dictionary continues to be the Society's best-selling volume. In the tribute to the great lexicographer at the 1935 Annual General Meeting the Society's debt to his work, 'to which it owes much of its prestige', was rightly emphasised. The terms of this tribute were composed by the Society's longtime Hon. Secretary and founder member, Eleanor Hull, in the week preceding her own death in January 1935.[137] The 'tact, firmness and decision', which had made her an ideal secretary, were singled out for mention in the report on her contribution to the Society at the same meeting.

Later in the same year it was decided to appoint a Dublin representative (14.5.1935) and Gerard Murphy, who was then working on Part 3 of *Duanaire Finn,* agreed to take up the position. Among many suggestions made by him concerning publications was a supplementary series containing extracts from earlier volumes (25.7.1935). This was agreed upon and Murphy was appointed general editor but the series never got off the ground.[138]

---

136 For the story of the Supplement, see below at p. 101.

137 This emerges from a talk on the Society, given in Irish about 1947/8, by M. O'Connell, a copy of which is now kept in Cork Public Museum (#AQNO= 1995/48, p. 17).

138 For a note on the original letter from Murphy, see at p. 95 below.

Among the regular volumes in progress during this period was *Duanaire Finn*, the second part of which was published in 1933. Paul Walsh had been asked by Council to edit this volume (25.1.1930), only to discover almost immediately that Gerard Murphy had already been working on it for several years (27.3.1930).[139] An edition of Amhlaoibh Ó Súileabháin's diary was first offered to the Society by D. J. O'Sullivan (25.1.1930) who was later replaced by the eventual editor, Michael McGrath (10.2.1934). The decision to invite McGrath to act as editor did not satisfy everyone. Council learned at its meeting of 15.10.1934 that Séamus Ó Casaide, who had previously edited extracts from the text in *Gadelica*, had attacked its decision in the *Irish Book Lover*. T. F. O'Rahilly's edition of translations of Spanish Tales continued to occupy much space in the minutes (14.2.1931, 20.3.1933, 14.5.1935).

Unlike the First World War, which scarcely affected the activities of the Society, the Second disrupted them considerably.[140] Already in 1939 the Chairman of Council, Robin Flower, had moved with the British Museum manuscripts to Aberystwyth. Similarly, the Hon. Treasurer, M. C. Lynch, who was a senior civil servant, had been forced to leave London for Llandudno. Attendance of Council members at meetings having thus been rendered extremely difficult, Maurice O'Connell asked of each by letter, dated 5.11.1940, 'to be allowed to carry on ordinary business' on his own. Publication continued until 1941 when Part 4 of *Lebor Gabála Érenn* was issued. Many volumes were, however, delayed by the War, most notably Part 3 of *Duanaire Finn* which was being printed in Belgium.

Soon after its establishment in 1940 the Dublin Institute for Advanced Studies was mentioned in the minutes in connexion with payment for its purchase of the volumes published by the Society (13.2.1943).

139 For an account of what had happened, see below at p. 94.

140 O'Connell vividly described the situation then obtaining in a letter, dated 1.11.1969, now in Cork Public Museum (# AQNO= 1995:5/61). Towards the end of the War, he states, 'we held the A.G.M. in the Gaelic League Office, or what was left of it, the windows had all gone'.

Box 4	ITS MB 8	12.2.1944-19.11.1966

A large ledger of 244 pages, bound in half leather and marbled boards. As in the previous minute book, the preliminary pages contain an index of contents. The minutes in this volume were kept by Maurice O'Connell until 20.3.1965 when, after 37 years as Hon. Secretary, he indicated his wish to resign. According to the minute, written by O'Connell himself, the news was greeted 'with silence' which shows that tensions had arisen between the Secretary and Council.[141] Kathleen Coady then took over the Secretaryship but soon resigned, forcing O'Connell to keep the minutes until the 1967 Annual General Meeting when a successor and namesake, Noel O'Connell, was appointed.[142] The latter had joined Council in 1958 and had previously acted as Hon. Treasurer. Maurice O'Connell finished what he had wrongly imagined to be his last minute on 20.3.1965 with the quatrain beginning: *Finis dár scríobhas ariamh go fóill.* A subsequent invitation to write a history of the Society was greeted with the comment that he had already been gathering material towards it in collaboration with K. Coady (17.7.1965). The tension between him and Council surfaced again in relation to a meeting planned for Dublin on 27.4.1968. Failure to hold the meeting led to his insisting on having a minute of censure retrospectively recorded on 9.11.1968 and signed by M. Dillon, President of the Society. O'Connell's aim, at least latterly, had been to move the Society to Dublin which, he felt, would lead to an increase in its membership and give it a higher profile (5.3.1966). Dillon, on the other hand, according to O'Connell, wanted 'to keep the Society as far away from Dublin as possible'.[143]

Robin Flower chaired his last meeting of Council on 25.11.1944. On 14.7.1945, after more than thirty years of service as Chairman of Council, he tendered his resignation on grounds of continuing illness. Very much against Council's wishes, but at his own insistence,

141 Cf. below at p. 103.

142 The last sixteen pages of the minutes, covering the period from 17.7.1965 to 19.11.1966, are prefaced by a note in O'Connell's hand which reads: 'The remaining pages of this book ... were written by Kathleen Coady and Maurice O'Connell. Kathleen Coady resigned after page 6 was done and M. O. C. carried on until the next AGM when Noel O'Connell was made Hon. Secretary in 1967'.

143 Cork Public Museum #AQNO = 1995:5/43. In this letter, dated 19.10.1968, O'Connell claims also to know the reason why Dillon opposed the move to Dublin but does not divulge it.

Flower's resignation was accepted on 17.11.1945. His death in the following January was noted in the minutes of the February meeting and, at the 1946 Annual General Meeting, a fitting tribute was paid to him by his successor as Chairman, A. Martin Freeman. Later in the same year, 23.11.1946, Council decided to ask Flower's daughter, Barbara, to hand over the Blasket volume to Professor Delargy for the Irish Folklore Commission.

Following the death in 1949 of the Society's first President, Douglas Hyde, T. F. O'Rahilly was elected to succeed him. The Presidency was still very much an honorary position and Council meetings were now presided over by Flower's successor as Chairman, A. Martin Freeman. The Presidency continued to be honorary in character under O'Rahilly's successor, Gerard Murphy, but this changed on his death with the appointment of Myles Dillon (24.8.1959) who had joined the Society almost thirty years previously (25.1.1930). Dillon's first meeting of Council, which coincided with the minuting of the death of A. Martin Freeman (12.3.1960), also marked the beginning of a policy of active involvement of Presidents which has continued under all his successors. He also introduced an era of cooperation with the Dublin Institute for Advanced Studies (24.8.1959), and his decision to waive the editor's honorarium of £100 for Volume 46 (*Lebor na Cert*) set a precedent of non-payment of editors that appears to have been followed ever since.

Among volumes in preparation at this time was a Supplement to Dinneen's Dictionary for which, on the recommendation of James Delargy, Thomas Waldron (Tomás de Bhaldraithe) was initially invited to act as editor (23.11.1946). At that stage, however, there was already mention of the Department of Education's project for a new dictionary, 'based on Dinneen' (30.4.1947).[144] L. S. Gogan agreed to edit the Supplement at a fee of £250 (12.2.1949) but some years later a decision was taken at Council 'not to press for completion of the Supplement' and 'to concentrate on getting its money back' (7.5.1955).[145] Another volume fated never to be completed was an edition of *Páirlement Chloinne Tomáis* which H. R. McAdoo began in 1940. David Greene's assumption of the editorship of this volume was

144 This was eventually published in 1977 as *Foclóir Gaeilge-Béarla* with Niall Ó Dónaill as editor. The Irish Texts Society is listed among the acknowledgements.

145 See also below at p. 99.

minuted on 30.3.1945.[146]

T. D. Fitzgerald, who had served on Council for 44 years (1920-63), and had acted as Secretary for ten (1918-28), died in December 1963. A lengthy appreciation of his contribution to the Society and especially of his role in the publication of the Dictionary, was written by Maurice O'Connell for the minutes of 10.3.1964.

Box 4 ITS MB 9 29.4.1967-6.11.1971

61 loose pages. The minutes are by Noel O'Connell, except those of the Dublin meeting of 20.5.1967, held in the Irish Folklore Commission, 82 Stephen's Green, which were written by Maurice O'Connell. This was the first meeting of Council ever held outside London; Myles Dillon occupied the Chair and Maurice O'Connell, having been asked to speak on the history of the Society, read the report of the Inaugural General Meeting. The 1968 Annual General Meeting, which marked the seventieth anniversary of the Society, was also held in Dublin and among those who attended was the President of Ireland, Éamon de Valera.[147] Myles Dillon addressed the meeting, concluding with the following words: 'After 70 years we are still full of purpose. The next 30 years – to make 100 – will bring us nearer our goal'.[148] Alas, of seven volumes mentioned as being then 'in the programme' only one was ever completed, albeit outside the Society's series of publications.[149]

The list of the Society's publications came up for discussion on 14.3.1970 when it was decided to have it revised with 'necessary spelling corrections'. No action appears, however, to have been taken and the revision was only recently completed in the 1997 Objects of the Society.

146 This text has since been edited elsewhere by N. J. A. Williams, *Pairlement Chloinne Tomáis* (Dublin, 1981).

147 See also below at p. 103.

148 The text of Professor Dillon's address is among the materials in Box 21 below at p. 103.

149 This was *Aislinge Meic Conglinne*, edited by Kenneth Jackson, which was published in 1990 by the Dublin Institute for Advanced Studies.

The Consultative Committee, which had been a feature of the Society since its foundation, was abolished on the 30.3.1968.[150]

The death of Maurice O'Connell, Secretary of the Society for 37 years, was noted with a sense of profound loss in the minutes for 28.5.1971. Minute books 7 and 8 bear eloquent witness to his 'many years of loyal and devoted service in maintaining and strengthening the Society'.

Box 5	ITS MB 10	4.3.1972-30.5.1981

154 loose pages. The minutes were kept by Noel O'Connell. Myles Dillon's unexpected death in June 1972 was reported to the meeting of 25.11.1972 and Idris Foster, who was then elected President, spoke at length of his predecessor's work for the Society.

At this stage the composition of the present Council was beginning to take shape. D. Ellis Evans, who succeeded Idris Foster in the Presidency, holding it between 1984 and 1992, joined Council in 1979. Some years earlier, in 1976, the current President, Pádraig Ó Riain, had become a member of Council, and the current Hon. Treasurer, M. J. Burns, attended his first meeting on 2.5.1981. The now longest standing member of Council, Bearnard Ó Dubhthaigh, was elected in 1971.

The provision of new introductions for volumes already published, which, since B. Bradshaw's appointment as Hon. Editor, has come to be an important component of the Society's publications, began to be discussed in 1973; Rachel Bromwich indicated her willingness to write a new Introduction to Volume 2, should it be reprinted (19.5.1973).

A new Book Distibution Centre about to be established in Dublin by Bord na Gaeilge is mentioned in the minutes of 23.9.1978. This is the present ÁIS agency which now handles the distribution of all the Society's publications.

150 It is clear from Cork Public Museum #AQNO – 1995:5/61, p. 5, that M O'Connell opposed this decision.

Box 5 ITS MB 11 18.7.1981-26.5.1987

115 loose pages, with pp. 111-5 blank. The first 43 pages are taken up with reports of Annual General Meetings for the period 1971-86. The minutes of Council meetings are on pp. 44-110. Both sets of minutes were kept by Noel O'Connell. During this period two meetings were held outside London, in Dublin on 17. 10. 1981 and in Cork on 25.9.1982. At both meetings the President, Professor Idris Foster, lectured on the history of the Society.[151] A decision at the Cork meeting that the Irish version of the Society's name be modernised to read *Cumann na Scríbheann Gaeilge* was rescinded at the 1983 Annual General Meeting because of lack of support.

The fiftieth anniversary of the death of Fr Dinneen was marked by a commemorative lecture by Noel O'Connell on 29.9.1984.[152] (The importance of Dinneen's Dictionary to the Society is reflected in the fact that it has been reprinted no fewer than nine times.) Many volumes were reprinted during this period which saw the emergence of the current policy of the Society, guided largely by M. J. Burns, of keeping all of its publications in print. The reprint that took up most space in the minutes was that of Keating's History of Ireland or *Foras Feasa ar Éirinn* which was provided with a new introduction, the first of a series now mainly subsumed into the Subsidiary Series, by Breandán Ó Buachalla.[153] The cost of this reprint was greatly defrayed by a very generous subvention from Allied Irish Banks (30.5.1987).[154]

Among new volumes proposed during this period and subsequently published were Ian Hughes's *Irish Gospel of Nicodemus* (17.10.1981), Anne O'Sullivan's *Poems on Marcher Lords* (19.11.1983),[155] and M. Herbert and P. Ó Riain's *Betha Adamnáin: the Irish Life of Adamnán* (19.10.1985). The news that a specially bound copy of a much earlier volume, J. Carney's *The Poems of Blathmac Son of Cú Brettan and the*

151 He also lectured on the history of the Society at the 1978 AGM, which marked the 80th anniversary of the Society.

152 The lecture was subsequently published by the Society under the title *Father Dinneen-his Dictionary & the Gaelic Revival.*

153 This was also published separately under the title *Foras Feasa ar Éirinn History of Ireland: Foreword to 1987 Reprint.*

154 See also above at p. 60.

155 On the death of the editor, noted by Council with regret on 29.9.1984, the volume was prepared for publication by P. Ó Riain, with the co-operation of William O'Sullivan.

Irish Gospel of Thomas, published in 1964, had been presented to and accepted by the Pope was announced at the Council meeting of 20.2.1982.

Professor Foster announced to Council his decision to retire from the Presidency on 25.6.1983 and was succeeded at the AGM that followed by Professor Ellis Evans.

Box 5 ITS MB (Rough Notes)

Two note books of 110 and 118 pages respectively are preserved containing rough notes of meetings kept by Maurice O'Connell for the periods 4.10.1937-12.2.1944 and 12.2.1949-10.3.1956. Among items of interest in these are several drafts of letters to editors and printers. One note book of 80 leaves used by Noel O'Connell to take notes at meetings between 29.9.1984 and 7.5.1989 is also preserved.

Boxes 6-13 Correspondence regarding Volumes

The surviving correspondence concerning individual volumes is mainly between the Secretary of the Society and either editors and printers or binders. Occasionally, however, letters from third parties bearing on particular volumes are also preserved. Some of these are from members of the Consultative Committee, such as T. F. O'Rahilly who, because of his friendship with Robin Flower, was often called upon for advice concerning volumes. Unfortunately, no correspondence at all concerning Volumes 1-18, which were published during Eleanor Hull's tenure of the post of Secretary, is preserved in the Society's archives.[156]

Box 6 Volumes 19-27

The publication of Douglas Hyde's edition of *Gabháltais Shearluis Mhóir* (Vol. 19) was followed by correspondence with Séamus Ó Casaide, whose address was then (27.6.1919) at Gleanntán (Glounthane), Cork, concerning errors of detail. (Hyde, writing from Frenchpark, admitted to the errors.) The correspondence regarding

156 There may be some among the papers of Eleanor Knott deposited in the National Library of Ireland.

Iomarbhágh na bhFileadh (Vols. 20-1) is with binders only. Five postcards from Eleanor Knott to T. D. Fitzgerald, mainly about the delay in printing, are all that survive in connexion with *A bhFuil Aguinn dár Chum Tadhg Dall Ó hUiginn* (Vols. 22-3). No correspondence has been preserved concerning C. O'Rahilly's edition of *Tóruigheacht Gruaidhe Griansholus* (Vol. 24), and, excepting some copies of reviews and an offprint, this is also true of W. Wulff's edition of *Rosa Anglica* (Vol. 25). Correspondence concerning S. H. O'Grady's edition of *Caithréim Thoirdhealbhaigh* (Vols. 26-7), although mainly with printers, includes letters from Robin Flower, who saw the work through the press, Eleanor Hull, and G. H. Orpen. The correspondence dates from 1915 to 1929, at which latter date Maurice O'Connell had just succeeded T. D. Fitzgerald as Secretary.

Boxes 7, 8 Volumes 28, 43

As is clear from the extensive correspondence concerning it, the preparation of *Duanaire Finn* Part 2 (Vol. 28) was not without incident. Gerard Murphy, who wrote from Altartote, Clones, Co. Monaghan, had been under the impression since 1922 that he was to edit this volume. One can imagine his surprise, therefore, when he learned from the *Irish Independent* of 27.1.1930 that the Society had invited Paul Walsh to act as editor. The misunderstanding appears to have been brought about by Eoin Mac Neill's failure to inform the Society of his arrangement with Murphy, but in any case Walsh agreed to step aside, thus paving the way for one of the Society's most successful collaborations with editors. The extensive correspondence relating to *Duanaire Finn* Part 3 (Vol. 43), mostly between Maurice O'Connell and Gerard Murphy, but also including communications with the Belgian printers and with other interested parties, covers the period 1933 to 1954. As is clear from its title page, several other scholars were also involved in the preparation of this volume, including Anne Cronin who corrected proofs variously in Dublin, Sweden, and Paris, and who spent many hours working on the Index. Risteárd Ó Foghladha was given the task of typing the text. Printing of the volume was held up by the War and, as this approached an end in 1944, the Department of External Affairs ascertained that the type still stood. Paul Grosjean became involved at this point and a letter from him to O'Connell, dated 25.9.1945, imparts some interesting information concerning his own wartime activities. He wrote: 'I was deciphering enemy messages as they came by radio. I succeeded (partly) and was not caught, in spite of the fact that the German police had every opportunity of giving me hell and shortness of life (in that order, thank God: the Irish saints usually promised them to their foes in the reverse order)'. A letter from Murphy to O'Connell, dated 6.11.1944, explains why Nessa Doran's (Ní Shéaghdha's) 'first class edition' of *Tóruigheacht Dhiarmada agus Ghráinne* (Vol. 48) was refused by the Dublin Institute for Advanced Studies. Also, in a letter dated 25.7.1935, Murphy asks the Society to consider 'running a supplementary series of 3/6 [three shillings and sixpence] books in a small format and similar binding to their main series ... with vocabularies instead of translations'.[157]

Box 9 Volumes 30-3, 34 (35, 39, 41, 44), 36, 37 (40), 38

Apart from a single letter from the editor little survives in the file concerning *Cinnlae Amhlaoibh Uí Shúileabháin* (Vols. 30-3).[158] That relating to *Lebor Gabála Érenn* (Vols. 34, 39, 41, 44) is much more substantial, with correspondence extending from 1938 to 1956. Included are some letters to the Secretary from R. A. S. Macalister, but the file mostly consists of letters from the printers and from Brian A. Riley, the 'educated reader' who, as its prescript states, saw Part 5 of the text through the press. The file on *Sgéalta Thomáis Uí Chathasaigh* (Vol. 36) is also quite extensive, with much discussion in letters from the editor, Douglas Hyde, written during the period 1937 to 1939, of such matters as the title of the book. Other aspects of the volume were of greater interest to other scholars. In a letter dated 24.11.1938, T. F. O'Rahilly, while singling out a lack of editors as the Society's main problem, also questioned the wisdom of publishing a folklore collection which might be best left to the Folklore Commission. (Another letter from Tadhg Ó Curnáin, a priest at Glengarrif who claimed not to be inspired by any *odium politicum*,

157 Cf. above at p. 86.

158 In a note by M. O'Connell, now Cork Public Museum #AQNO = 1995: 5/34, reference is made to 'two large packets of correspondence in Irish' from Fr McGrath still extant in 1968.

described Hyde's choice of tales as trash. Yet another, from An Seabhac, pointed to the non-folklore character of one of the tales.) Also included in this file are drafts of letters from M. O'Connell to J. G. O'Keeffe, Paul Grosjean, Tadhg Ó Donnchadha or Torna (in Irish), and É. O'Toole, asking for contibutions to a Dinneen Memorial Volume towards which Hyde and Freeman had already promised some material.[159] Both Grosjean (11.3.1937) and O'Keeffe (11.3.1937) excused themselves on grounds of ill health. Nothing of note survives in the sparse files of *Aithdioghluim Dána* (Vols. 37, 40) and *Stair Ercuil ocus a Bás* (Vol. 38).

Box 10 Volumes 42, 45, 46, 47, 49, 51, 52

The file on *Beatha Aodha Ruaidh Uí Dhomhnaill* (Vols. 42, 45) contains a few letters from Paul Walsh, dating to 1940, but mostly consists of correspondence with Colm O Lochlainn, dating from 1941 to 1956 and relating to the progress of the work through the press. From now on the correspondence in the files is mainly with printers, such as the Oxford University Press in relation to *Lebor na Cert* (Vol. 46), Dublin University Press in connexion with *The Poems of Giolla Brighde Mac Conmidhe* (Vol. 51), and the Leinster Leader concerning *Cath Maige Tuired* (Vol. 52). The file on *The Poems of Blathmac* (Vol. 47) is non-existent and that on *Táin Bó Cúalnge from the Book of Leinster* (Vol. 49) consists of two letters from Cecile O'Rahilly.

Box 11 Volumes 53, 54, 55, 56, 57

A few letters from editors and very little else survives in the files of *Poems on Marcher Lords* (Vol. 53), *Betha Adamnáin* (Vol. 54), and *Stair Nicoméid* (Vol. 55). No files are present for *Oidheadh Chloinne hUisneach* (Vol. 56) and *Beatha Bharra* (Vol. 57).

Box 12 Proposed but Unpublished Volumes 1-10

These files consist of correspondence concerning volumes offered to the Society but never published under its auspices, either because the editions were deemed to be unacceptable or, much more commonly,

159 See below at p. 99.

because editors never completed them; less usually, volumes might also have been taken to other publishers. The files are presented in the chronological order of their appearance in the publishing programme of the Society.

1. An edition of Translations of Spanish Tales offered in 1909 by T. F. O'Rahilly has the distinction of having been one of the longest standing uncompleted volumes in the programme of the Society; it left O'Rahilly's hands in 1935 for those of Éamonn O'Toole only to be returned unfinished in 1938.[160]
2. The greater part of the correspondence concerning the O'Neill Poems, including letters to the Secretary from the editor, Tadhg Ó Donnchadha (Torna), from Robin Flower who was assisting with the translations into English, and from the O'Neill in Lisbon who took a particular interest in the project and contributed £20 towards its cost in 1913, dates to between 1919 and 1925. The Poems were finally published without translation by the Irish Manuscripts Commission in 1931.[161]
3. In 1916 Margaret Browne, who had completed an M. A. under Bergin and Hyde, offered an edition of the Life of Mac Creiche.[162]
4. Several letters from Tomás Ó Máille, written over a long period (1918-34), deal among other matters with the possibility of editions of the Poems of Eochaidh Ó hEodhasa by Ó Máille himself, of the Poems of Eoghan Ruadh Mac an Bhaird by Tomás Ó Raghallaigh,[163] of poems by the Mac Craith Poets by Tomás Ó Conaill, and of the Poems of Gofraidh Fionn Ó Dálaigh by A. Walsh.
5. A few letters, dated 1925-6, relating to the prospect of an edition by Elizabeth Aughney of the Irish translation of the Middle-English Romance, William of Palermo.[164] T. F. O'Rahilly had recommended the edition and a letter bearing on it from Douglas Hyde is also in the file.

160 See above at p. 81.

161 See above at p. 83.

162 See now C. Plummer, *Miscellanea Hagiographica Hibernica* (Brussels, 1925) 7-96.

163 See now T. Ó Raghallaigh, ed., *Duanta Eoghain Ruaidh Mhic An Bhaird* (Galway, 1930).

164 See now C. O'Rahilly, ed., *Eachtra Uilliam* (Dublin, 1949).

6. A file consisting mainly of correspondence with printers concerning the Blasket Volume planned by Robin Flower which was partly set up in type. The correspondence, which contains some letters from Flower, dates from 1928 to 1946 and closes with a letter from Séamus Ó Duilearga welcoming the suggestion that the volume be taken over by the Folklore Commission.[165]
7. Extensive correspondence, from the period 1930 to 1933, concerning a proposed edition of the Book of the Dean of Lismore by Neil Ross. The edition was supported by W. J. Watson but, in a letter to Robin Flower dated 20. 3. 1933, and written from his then home in Douglas, Cork, T. F. O'Rahilly advised 'bluntly and brutally' that it be rejected. In the same letter O'Rahilly announced that he had begun a new line of investigation on the question of the Goidelic invasion and of their predecessors in Ireland which he hoped to offer to the [British?] Academy and which, he believed, would be a starting point for future investigation of early Irish history.[166] He also spoke of his desire to return to Dublin and of his lack of rapport with Torna.
8. Extensive correspondence, beginning in 1931 and continuing until 1968, relating to the edition of an Irish translation of *Hortus Sanitatis Hibernicus*, the so-called Herbal Volume, by Winifred Wulff. This is easily the uncompleted volume which survived longest in the publishing programme of the Society. Initially the correspondence is mainly with W. Wulff who wrote on postcards. With the failure of Ms. Wulff's eyesight, Róisín Walsh became involved, together with Nessa Doran (Ní Shéaghdha) (1944-55). Later still an attempt was made to enlist the help of Máirín de Valera (1968).[167]
9. A few letters, dated 1934, relating to the possible edition of *Scél Shaltrach na Rann* by Myles Dillon for the Society.[168]
10. Letters, dated 1934, relating to the possibility of a volume being edited for the Society by Liam S. Gogan.

---

165 See now R. Flower, S. Ó Duilearga, ed., *Seanchas ón Oileán Tiar* (Dublin, 1956).

166 *The Goidils and their Predecessors* was published by the British Academy in 1936.

167 The last name to be mentioned in connexion with the editing of this volume was Bearnard Ó Dubhthaigh who, according to a letter by Maurice O'Connell (Cork Public Museum #AQNO = 1995:5/61), had agreed to carry on with the work.

168 Subsequently edited by Dillon in *Celtica* 4 (1958) 1-43.

Box 13 Proposed but Unpublished Volumes 11-16

11. A few letters, dated 1934, involving J. G. O'Keeffe and A. Martin Freeman and concerning the continuation of a volume of Apocryphal Texts originally offered by Robin Flower.[169]
12. Letters, dated 1935, on the prospect of a Genealogical Volume edited by Kathleen Mulchrone.
13. A file relating to a planned volume in memory of P. S. Dinneen for which offers of editions of texts had come from Douglas Hyde (*Stair na Lombardach*) and A. Martin Freeman (Dialogue between Soul and Body). The file also contains a letter from Torna, who had been invited to contribute, complaining of the 'old fashioned rule' requiring a translation into English of the text.
14. A letter from Mícheál Mac Craith S. J., dated 1937, offering an edition of a Roman Missal in Royal Irish Academy Manuscript 24 L 19. According to a draft reply at back of letter the offer was refused as unsuitable for the series.
15. Correspondence, extending from 1940 to 1951, relating to the preparation of an edition of *Páirlement Chloinne Tomáis* by H. R. McAdoo (1940-46), whose work was very much impeded by the restrictions in place during the War; his successor as editor, David Greene (1946-51), appears also to have made little progress. McAdoo's typed description of the 'Contents' of the volume is included in the file.[170]
16. A letter from Alan Bruford, dated 26.3.1968, in connexion with a proposed edition of a text dealing with Conall Gulban.[171]

Box 14 Dinneen File 1

Included in this file are several batches of correspondence relating mainly to the enlarged Dictionary published in 1927. The file begins with letters exchanged in 1917-19 between members of Council, T. D. Fitzgerald, E. Hull, and T. A. England, concerning the Agreement to be signed with Dinneen; the signed Agreement, dated 1.9.1919, is also

169 See also n. 133 above.

170 See also p. 89 above.

171 According to a letter preserved among the effects of Maurice O'Connell in Cork Public Museum #AQNO = 1995:5/61) Bruford had been recommended as editor by Séamus O Duilearga.

contained in the file. There follow two batches of very substantial correspondence, mainly between T. D. Fitzgerald and Dinneen, about the progress of the Dictionary, covering the periods 1917-22 and 1923-27. The latter batch contains, among many other items of interest, a detailed list of payments to Dinneen from 1918 to 1925 and a copy of the original form of dedication proposed by Dinneen in a letter dated 19.5.1927. This dedication, of which Council was prepared to publish the first part only, reads in full: *Do Phádraig mhac Calprainn aspal agus éarlamh Éireann an foillsiughadh so ar an gcruth atá i ndiu tar éis gach cruadhtan is cruaidhbheart ar an nGaedhealghlór a bhí 'na bhéal as 'na chluaisaibh* (sic) *míle go leith éigean bliadhan ó shoin i dTeamhair na Ríogh.* Also included in this file are various documents relating to the Guarantee Fund established to help defray the considerable cost of the Dictionary, including a copy of the original printed appeal for support published in 1918.[172]

Box 15 Dinneen File 2

This file is given over to the extensive correspondence conducted by Council with successive Ministers of Education in Dublin concerning grants towards the cost of, and rights to ownership of, the Dictionary. The correspondence had already begun in 1921 with Seán Ua Ceallaigh (Sceilg), Minister of Education of Dáil Éireann, and continued with Free State Ministers, including Eoin Mac Neill, between 1923-26. At a later stage, 1945-47, there was considerable correspondence with the Department, conducted mainly through the Irish High Commissioner in London, concerning the possible acquisition by the Irish Government of the Society's rights to the Dictionary. Later still, in 1959-60, correspondence ensued about the possibility of the Department buying what was ready of the Supplement to Dinneen's Dictionary prepared by L. S. Gogan, with a view to its inclusion in the Department's own Irish-English Dictionary.[173] Also contained in this file is a record of the correspondence with Dinneen's relatives and their legal representatives after the lexicographer's death in 1934 on the subject of royalties.

172 See above at p. 82.

173 See also below in Dinneen File 3. Among the acknowledgements in *Foclóir Gaeilge-Béarla,* edited by Niall Ó Dónaill and published by the Irish Government in 1977, is one to the Irish Texts Society for permission to use Dinneen's Dictionary. No reference is made, however, to the Supplement.

Box 16 Dinneen File 3

On the 13.12.1935 Éamon de Valera addressed the Inaugural Meeting of the Gaelic Society of the National University at U.C.D. Risteárd Ó Foghladha, who was present, wrote to Maurice O'Connell, Secretary of the Irish Texts Society, on the following day to say that, among other matters, de Valera had stated that 'he would like to see a new edition of Dinneen's Dictionary'. As is clear from various earlier minutes,[174] and also from letters addressed among others to Tomás Ó Deirg, Minister for Education and Vice-President of the Society,[175] in 1934-5, Council had by then already begun to explore the possibility of publishing a Supplement to the Dictionary. To judge, however, by correspondence with Andreas O'Keeffe, dating mainly to the years 1936-9, the exact state of the papers left by Dinneen, many of which were in the possession of his collaborator, L. S. Gogan, in the National Museum, had first to be established.

After the War the matter of the Supplement was pursued with renewed vigour and considerable correspondence survives from 1946 to 1948 on the question of a possible editor. Letters from Francis Shaw, L. McKenna, and J. H. Delargy contain advice on this question. Tomás de Bhaldraithe showed great interest in the project in a long letter, dated 9.11.1946, in which he also outlined his views on which categories of words the Dictionary should contain. In 1948, however, he finally declined an invitation to edit the Supplement.

Correspondence with L. S. Gogan, who had co-operated with Dinneen on the 1927 Dictionary, began in 1949 and an Agreement between him and Council for the production of a Supplement of roughly 200 pages was drawn up and signed on 21.2.1951. By 23.10.1953 he was in a position to send to Council four specimen printed pages now contained in the file. By 1955 difficulties with the editor, which had been threatening from the beginning, had led almost to litigation and, with one-third of the Supplement apparently complete, the arrangements with Gogan were cancelled.[176]

---

174 See above at p. 86.

175 See above at p. 69.

176 As the file in Box 15 shows, some effort was made to persuade the Irish Government to take over what was ready of the Supplement for use in connexion with Ó Dónaill's Dictionary. According to a minute for 12.3.1960 negotiations between the Society, Gogan and the Government were then still in progress.

Box 17 Dinneen File 4

This file consists mainly of correspondence with the Department of Education, extending from 1969 to 1978, concerning the possibility of a grant towards the reprinting of the Dictionary. Also in the file are letters from the Society's printers/publishers on the subject of the small (1916) and enlarged (1922-8) Dictionaries.

Box 18 General Correspondence 1 (1909-1948)

Some correspondence of a general nature with fellow members of Council, with ordinary members of the Society, or with libraries, has also been preserved. Included in this file is a collection of letters from Douglas Hyde, written mainly in Irish in the years 1919-24. One letter, dated 16.1.1920, reports the appointment of J. Pokorny, then 'dying of hunger in Vienna', to succeed K. Meyer in Berlin. Another, dated 27.8.1921, pleads for Dr Ludwig Mühlhausen who was afraid that, as a German, he might not be acceptable as a member of the Society. Also in this batch is a letter written by T. D. Fitzgerald to Hyde in 1919, together with a reply from Hyde, concerning the efforts of the former to secure an M. A. in Irish as an external student. A letter from P. S. Ó Móráin, dated 13.8.1920, discusses an attempt by Piaras Béaslaí to unseat Sceilg (Seán Ua Ceallaigh) as President of the Gaelic League. Also of interest is a twelve-page manuscript history of the Society, originally written about 1930 as the text of a lecture, by Maurice O'Connell and updated in the 1950s.

Of particular importance for the history of the Society is the correspondence relating to the War years 1939-45 when it became impossible to hold regular meetings. The particularly difficult year of 1941 accounts for most of the correspondence. A long letter from Robin Flower, who, having spent the greater part of the War years in Aberystwyth, returned to London in 1944, is of particular interest for the information it provides about the state of his health among other matters. Dated 25.7.1944, it also refers to the frequency with which 'doodle bugs' were then falling near his home in Southgate.

There is no correspondence on the subject of the Society's 50th anniversary in 1948, which, perhaps because of its closeness to the end of the War, does not appear to have been commemorated.[177]

177 The minutes of the period are also silent on the question.

Boxes 19, 20 General Correspondence (1949-56, 1957-60)

These boxes contain a miscellaneous collection of M. O'Connell's correspondence as Secretary, sometimes with members of Council (A. Martin Freeman, M. C. Lynch), more often with ordinary members and libraries. Included is the letter of acceptance written by T. F. O'Rahilly on 4.9.1950 in response to the invitation to become President of the Society.

Box 21 General Correspondence (1961-68)

The contents of this box include documents relating to the seventieth anniversary meeting of the Society held in Dublin on 27.4.1968. Among the attendance was the President of Ireland, Éamon de Valera. The background correspondence of the meeting, consisting mainly of letters, or drafts of letters, to and from M. O'Connell, throws a good deal of light on the internal politics of Council. O'Connell was afraid that M. Dillon, who had secured the election to Council of R. Bromwich, Idris Foster and Kenneth Jackson, was about to take the running of the Society out of Irish hands.[178]

Also contained in this box are some documents from 1965-6 relating to the rules of the Society.

Boxes 22-8 General Correspondence (1969-)

These boxes contain the correspondence as Secretary of Noel O'Connell. This consists mainly of communications concerning membership lists, enquiries from individual members, often about the difficulty of obtaining volumes, searches for volumes which had gone astray, problems arising with printers, arrangements for book launches, and sundry other business matters.

178 Further commentary on these matters is contained in O'Connell's papers in Cork Public Museum #AQNO = 1995:5/41.

CHAPTER SEVEN

Minutes of the Sub-Committee, Provisional Committee, and Inaugural General Meeting[179]

ORIGINAL 'PROVISIONAL COMMITTEE' 1896[180]

D. Comyn. Dr A. Colles. F. A. Fahy. T. J. Flannery. G. A. Greene. D. Hyde. P. W. Joyce. J. McNeill. J. G. O'Keeffe. Goddard Orpen. G. Sigerson.

ADDED BY THE GENERAL COMMITTEE[181] IN MAY 1897.

R. Barry O'Brien. R. Stewart Macalister. Norma Borthwick. Eleanor Hull. - O'Sullivan.[182]

THE TEXTS SOCIETY SUB-COMMITTEE MET ON MAY 24TH 1897.

There were present. Messrs. T. J. Flannery, Goddard Orpen, G. A. Greene, Dr A. Colles, R. Barry O'Brien, R. Stewart Macalister, J. G. O'Keeffe, Miss Borthwick and Miss Hull.

Mr. T. J.[183] Flannery having been re-elected as Chairman, Miss Borthwick and Miss Hull were appointed to act as Hon. secretaries and Mr. R. Stewart Macalister as Hon. Treasurer. Mr. Flannery then made a statement with regard to the present position of the Texts Society:

He said that copies of the first circular had been sent to all members of the ILS and a few to persons outside the Society both at home and

179 The annotation is by the editor.

180 Unfortunately, perhaps because Eleanor Hull was not a member, the minutes of the original Provisional Committee do not appear to have survived. Its Secretary, and Chairman, was T. J. Flannery.

181 This refers to the Irish Literary Society.

182 This is Michael O'Sullivan who signed his name to the list of those present at the second meeting of the Committee.

183 Written J. T.

abroad.[184] Out of these about 50 promises of support had been obtained. Promises of assistance in the editing of texts had also been received from Dr D. Hyde, Dr S. H. O'Grady, Dr Joyce and Mr. Comyn.

After several discussions on the whole subject, the secretaries were requested to communicate with the following publishers, Messrs. Duffy, Gill & Hodges & Figgis in Dublin and Messrs. Williams & Norgate, Keegan Paul & Co., Constable & Co. and David Nutt in London with a view to obtaining from them estimates of the cost of publication of the first number – size large 8vo in paper covers.[185] The Text in Irish type with English translation on opposite page. Brief introduction and a few notes on archaisms etc. at the end. Edition of *500*. Mr. O'Sullivan was then elected on the Committee.

T. J. Flannery.[186]

The Committee met on June 2nd 1897.

Mr. T. J. Flannery in the Chair. Those present were: Norma Borthwick, H. Sec., M. O'Sullivan, R. A. Stewart Macalister, H. Treas., Goddard H. Orpen, G. A. Greene, Abraham Colles, Eleanor Hull, H. Sec.[187]

Miss Hull reported the result of an interview with Archibald Constable & Co. and with a representative of the firm of Keegan Paul & Co. A letter was also read from Gill & Sons Printers Dublin enclosing an estimate for printing and publication of proposed text. The other publishers awaited further information before supplying the required estimates.

Letters were read from Drs. Joyce, Hyde, Sigerson, Prof. Kuno Meyer, Mr. McNeill and Mr. Comyn expressing sympathy with the projects of the Committee and making some valuable suggestions. Miss Hull reported that Dr S. H. O'Grady would probably be able to turn his attention to the editing of a text for the Society in the Autumn and Dr D. Hyde promised to edit two texts, probably giving the first one next year. He suggested *Eactra Ghiolla an Fiugha* as the text he

184 14 copies of the Appeal survive among Eoin Mac Neill's papers in the National Library (MS 10,881, folder 18). I owe this information to Pádraigín Riggs.

185 In fact, hard covers were used for all volumes.

186 Signature of Chairman.

187 All these names were signed by the individuals themselves.

would first take up.[188] Mr. Flannery also kindly offered to edit a text for the Society.[189]

It was resolved that the texts should be published with as few corrections or emendations as possible and that as soon as three or four texts had been decided upon and editors found, a new circular should be issued. Mr. G. A. Greene reminded the Committee that the General Committee had agreed to pay the expenses of this forthcoming circular out of the general funds of the Society.

The Secretaries were directed to write to Father Hickey of Maynooth, Prof. B. O'Looney, MRIA, Father O'Leary and others to ask if they would assist in the work of the Society as Editors: also to the secretaries of various archaeological and Gaelic societies etc. to acquire the number of their members and ask their co-operation in making the work of the Texts Society known, and circularising their members.

Abraham Colles

A COMMITTEE MEETING WAS HELD ON JUNE 15TH.

Present Dr Colles in the Chair, Mr. Macalister, Mr. R. B. O'Brien, Miss Hull, H. Sec.

Letters were read from Miss Borthwick, Mr. McNeill and others conveying suggestions about MSS. etc., also from Dr Hyde saying that he would undertake the editorship of the first volume for the Society and could have it ready by the end of next year. Letters were then read from various Societies complying with the requests of the Committee to have their forthcoming Circular inserted in their journals and papers. Several of these societies pressed for an immediate consignment of circulars to be sent out with their July magazines, but the Subcommittee after discussion decided to report to the General Committee that they were unable to prepare[190] the circular at such short notice. Publishers' Estimates were then presented, and a draft Circular, drawn up by Mr. Macalister, was discussed. A suggestion

188 This was published as Volume 1 of the Society's series.

189 At this time Flannery was working on an edition of the Life of Colum Cille, the 1300th anniversary of whose death fell in 1897. An update on his progress with the edition, which was never completed, was published in the First Annual Report.

190 Written over crossed out word.

was sent up to the General Committee that Mr Lipton[191] should be approached with a view to obtaining help towards defraying the preliminary expenses of the Irish Texts Society.
G. A. Greene.[192]

A COMMITTEE MEETING WAS HELD ON OCTOBER 15TH.
Present: Mr. Greene in the Chair, Mr. O'Keeffe, Mr. O'Sullivan, Dr Colles, Miss Borthwick and Miss Hull, Hon. Secs., Mr. Macalister, Hon. Treas.

The *Daily Chronicle* correspondence on the subject of the Irish Text Society was read, and the position to be taken up by the Text Committee with regard to Mr. Nutt's proposals was discussed at some length.[193] Letters were read from Mr. Nutt and Dr Hyde upon the subject, but a decision was postponed until the next committee: Miss Hull being instructed in the meantime, to communicate with Sealy, Bryers and Walker and with the London Book Depot[194], to enquire on what terms they would print and distribute the volumes of the Irish Texts Society if the Committee retained the publishing of the vols. in their own hands. Letters were read from Mr. Brian O'Looney offering his services as one of the editors of the Society,[195] and from Mr. Russell[196] and Mr. Olden[197] conveying suggestions. The question of price of books and subscriptions was then discussed, and a suggestion was made that one extra vol. of the series should occasionally be published suitable for the use of students under the Intermediate Education Board.
Danl. Mescal, Chairman

---

191 Thomas J. Lipton, successful businessman, was of Irish descent.

192 Signature of Chairman.

193 A copy of a letter by Alfred Nutt to the editor of the *Daily Chronicle* on the subject of the publication of Irish texts was reprinted, and provided with a long commentary, in the August 1897 issue of *Irisleabhar na Gaedhilge* (pp. 59-61).

194 It was this firm that published T. J. Flannery's 1896 edition of *Oisín in the Land of Youth*.

195 O'Looney (Ó Luanaigh) was by then almost seventy and died three years later before he could complete any editorial work for the Society.

196 This is doubtless Thomas O'Neill Russell († 1908), the editor of a modern Irish version of *An Bhoramha Laighean* (Dublin, 1901). At this stage he was seventy years old.

197 Rev. Thomas Olden of Ballyclough, Mallow, Co. Cork, had edited a number of Irish texts, including a selection from the Würzburg glosses, *The Holy Scriptures in Ireland one Thousand Years Ago* (Dublin, 1888).

THE COMMITTEE MET ON OCT. 22ND, 1897.

Mr. Mescal in the Chair. Present, Mr. O'Keeffe, Mr. O'Sullivan, Mr. Macalister, Mr. Colles, Mr. Graves (Ex-officio)[198], Miss Hull & Miss Borthwick, Hon. Secs.

The Minutes having been read and signed, an estimate was presented from Messrs. Sealy, Bryers and Walker for printing. A letter was read from Dr Hyde advising the Committee to work with Mr. Nutt as publisher, both on the ground of his position as a publisher of Celtic work, and in consequence of the advantageous offer made to the society.[199] Miss Hull proposed and Mr. Macalister seconded the proposal that Mr. Nutt's offer be considered favourably[200] and this was carried. It was agreed to interview Mr. Nutt on the subject. The two alternative proposals made by Mr. Nutt were then discussed and it was agreed that the second should be considered,[201] i. e. the Committee of the Texts Society should become responsible for the raising[202] of funds and their distribution and keep the entire control of publications in their own hands; paying Mr. Nutt a commission of 10% on the published price of each volume. A section of the Sub-Committee, consisting of Messrs Mescal & O'Keeffe & Miss Hull & Miss Borthwick, were appointed to meet and confer with Mr. Nutt in order to report to the Committee.

Miss Borthwick then read a letter from Mr. Kerwick[203] advising that the subscription to the Society should not exceed 5/- and the Committee decided provisionally[204] that this would be its amount, but asking a higher subscription from those willing to assist the project for its own sake. Mr. Kerwick also suggested that where editors could not be paid, an offer should be made to paid copyists to relieve the editors of the labour of writing out the texts, the copyists being instructed to make no alterations whatever in the texts.

198 Graves was Secretary of the Irish Literary Society, whence the reference to his office.

199 A sentence is then crossed out.

200 Miss Hull first wrote 'accepted' but then crossed it out.

201 Written over crossed out word.

202 Written over crossed out word.

203 I have been unable to discover who Mr Kerwick was.

204 Added above line.

Miss Hull suggested that a list of patrons of the Society should be drawn up and scholars at home and abroad asked to become patrons of the society.[205]
Goddard H. Orpen[206]

THE SUB-COMMITTEE MET ON THURSDAY OCT 28TH.

Mr. Goddard Orpen in the Chair. Present Mr. O'Keeffe, Dr Colles, Mr. Macalister, Miss Hull, Hon. Sec.

Mr. O'Keeffe reported that Miss Borthwick, Miss Hull, Mr. Mescal & Mr. O'Keeffe had conferred with Mr. Nutt on the previous Monday on the nature of the texts to be undertaken by the Irish Texts Society and the terms of publication.

In accordance with the terms laid down in the preliminary circular, it was agreed that the texts published should be mainly modern, but that older texts should not be altogether[207] excluded from the scope of the Society's work. Mr. Nutt made some suggestions with regard to texts to be undertaken and editors.

The two schemes of publication were then discussed.

1st. If the Society wished to keep the entire control in their own hands, Mr. Nutt would publish at 10% commission on the net trade price. In this case the Society would bear the whole cost of production and advertising,[208] would find the subscribers, fix the price of each volume and rate at which it was to be sold. The cost of printing he estimated at about £57, binding at £12. 10 and commission on 500 copies of estimated size = £5. 10 making a total of about £75 on an edition of 500 copies.

2nd. Mr. Nutt was prepared to publish (including printing, binding, advertising, circularizing, insurance and warehousing) an edition of 500 copies of estimated size, provided the Society guarantee a list of 200 subscribers at 5/- or of any larger number at a reduced figure for any number above 200, Mr. Nutt distributing to such subscribers the volumes as published. Any profits accruing after the expenses have been covered to be divided as to 2/3rd to the Society and 1/3rd to Nutt.

205 This became the Society's Consultative Committee.
206 Signature of Chairman.
207 Added above line.
208 Followed by crossed out 'and publication'.

If this proposal were accepted, Mr. Nutt would desire to be consulted as regards the texts proposed to be published, but he would not interfere with any editor who wished to work with a free hand. All works sold to non-subscribers would be sold at a higher figure than the subscription price. It was resolved that the 2nd scheme should be recommended for adoption by the General Committee, but that the subscription should be fixed at 7/6, out of which Mr. Nutt will receive a proportion as stated above,[209] with a view of securing a sum to the Society out of which the outgoing expenses of Editors on behalf of the Society should be defrayed and where necessary, copyists engaged to work under their directions in the public libraries. The Society had in view the desirability of offering some remuneration to editors, if this should prove possible.[210]
Goddard H. Orpen[211]

THE SUB COMMITTEE MET ON THURSDAY NOV. 4TH, 1897.
Present, Mr. Goddard Orpen in the Chair, Mr. Graves (ex-officio), Mr. O'Keeffe, Mr. Macalister, Mr. O'Sullivan, Miss Borthwick & Miss Hull, Hon. Secs.

The Minutes having been read and signed, a draft Circular was read and amended for presentation to the General Committee - and a list of ancient and modern texts was prepared for insertion in the Circular.[212]
Goddard H. Orpen[213]

209 This clause is added above the line.

210 This became and remained the Society's practice, until it was discontinued during Myles Dillon's Presidency in the 1960s.

211 Signature of Chairman.

212 The appearance of this circular was described in *Irisleabhar na Gaedhilge* (January, 1898) as 'one of the events of the new year'. Two of the three volumes promised in the Circular, Hyde's 'romantic tales' and Comyn's *Foras Feasa*, were published as Volumes 1 and 4. The third, T. J. Flannery's edition of *Beatha Choluim Chille,* was never completed.

213 Signature of Chairman.

THE SUB-COMMITTEE MET ON MONDAY, NOV. 15, 1897.

Present, Mr. Goddard Orpen in the chair, Mr. O'Keeffe, Mr. Mescal, Miss Borthwick, Mr. O'Sullivan, Mr. Macalister.

The minutes having been read and signed, two letters from Mr. Hyde were read, referring principally to the pieces he proposes to edit. A letter was then read from Mr. Nutt, explaining his views as to the constitution of the Text[214] Society apart from the Irish Literary Society. A draft agreement sent by Mr. Nutt was read and discussed. With regard to clause 7 of this agreement, it was resolved that Mr. Nutt be told that it was never contemplated that the Text Society should be under any risk beyond furnishing 200 subscriptions (as stated in his letter of June 6th) and that he be asked to consent to the omission of clause 7 of the draft agreement.

A letter was read from Mr. Flannery, resigning his membership of the Text Committee, and enclosing a subscription from Miss MacManus of Worthing. It was proposed by Miss Borthwick, seconded by Mr. O'Keeffe, and unanimously agreed that Mr. Flannery's resignation be accepted with very great regret, and Miss Borthwick was directed to write to Mr. Flannery, expressing the regret of the Committee and thanking him for the promise of editing a text for the Society.

Goddard H. Orpen[215]

THE IRISH TEXTS COMMITTEE MET ON NOV. 26TH, 1897.

Present. Mr. Goddard Orpen in the Chair, Dr Colles, Mr. O'Keeffe, Miss Hull, Miss Borthwick and Mr. Macalister. The minutes having been signed, a letter from Mr. Nutt was read and his modifications of draft agreement were agreed to. These modifications were: withdrawal of Clause 7, raising of the guarantee limits from 200 to 250 and division of profits as to half to the Society and half to Nutt, all profits being subjected to a tax of 25% to form a reserve fund. It was resolved: (I) that a clause be added to the agreement giving either party power to determine agreement on one year's written notice. (II) That clause (4) be amended "at a price less than 10/- to private purchasers or 8/8 to trade purchasers". (III) That Clause (8) be amended

214 Above line.

215 Signature of Chairman.

"that Mr. Nutt shall be (ex officio) a member of the Council of the Irish Texts Society".

Letters were read from Mr. R. Wilson, Mr. Norman Moore,[216] Dr Joyce[217] and Mr. Trench. Mr. Wilson offered a donation to the initial expenses of the undertaking.

Some amendments were then made to the draft circular. Mr. Nutt's suggestions were discussed and in part incorporated into the draft.
Goddard H. Orpen[218]

THE TEXTS SUB-COMMITTEE MET ON THURSDAY 9TH DEC., 1897.

Present: Mr. G. Orpen in the Chair, Mr. Barry O'Brien, Dr Colles, Miss Borthwick, Miss Hull, Mr. O'Keeffe.

A letter was read from Mr. Nutt agreeing to the amendments in the Draft Agreement and promising a fresh copy within a few days which could be initialled by himself and representatives of the Irish Texts Subcommittee. Letters, suggesting amendments to the Draft Circular, were read from Dr Hyde, Mr. Flannery, Mr. Nutt and Mr. Comyn. The latter offered to edit for the Society Keating's *Foras Feasa ar Éirinn*.[219]

The circular was then revised. The most important of the amendments being the substitution of Mr. G. Orpen's name (as Chairman of the Provisional Committee) for that of Mr. B. O'Brien and Mr. Graves as officers of the ITS
Goddard H. Orpen

THE IRISH TEXTS SUBCOMMITTEE MET ON DEC. 17TH, 1897.

Present: Mr. Goddard Orpen (in the Chair), Mr. Macalister, Mr. Greene, Miss Hull & Miss Borthwick.

Miss Borthwick reported that the Committee[220] of the Irish Literary Society agreed to the omission of the names of Mr. Graves and Mr.

216 A medical doctor, Moore was also interested in Irish scholarship and history; he translated Windisch's *Concise Irish Grammar*.

217 This is presumably P. W. Joyce who was a member of the original Provisional Committee.

218 Signature of Chairman.

219 Comyn edited Part 1 of Keating's work for the Society (Volume 4).

220 Above line.

O'Brien from the Circular, but they hoped that some recognition of their initiation of the Scheme by the Irish Literary Society[221] would be made in the prefaces of the volumes issued by the Texts Society or in some other suitable manner.

The revised prospectus was gone through: it was agreed to add the names of the Provisional Committee as a heading to the Circular, and other slight amendments were agreed to.

Mr. Macalister having taken the second chair, it was agreed to send copies of the Circular to the Irish press and the literary papers.[222] Various suggestions were made about the mode of distribution and persons to whom the circulars should be sent. It was decided to ask Mr. Wilson to allow his promised subscription to go towards the expenses of postage and circularising.
Daniel Mescal Chairman.

LIST OF SOCIETIES ETC. TO WHOM CIRCULARS WERE SENT.[223]

To Mr. Alfred Nutt, 270 Strand, W. C., for private distribution – Folklore Society, and Zeitschrift für kelt. Philologie., 1500 copies. To Keegan Paul & Co., Paternoster House, Charing X. Road, 300 copies for Early English Text Society. Dr Furnival (Hon. Sec.), 3 St. Georges Sqr., Primrose Hill, N. W. To Philological Soc. of London, University College, Gower St., W. C., 100 copies (Dr Furnival, Hon. Sec.). To Gaelic Society of London, Crane Court, Fleet St., and Highland Societies, 100 copies. To Viking Club, 17 Grosvenor Road, Westminster, S. W., 200 copies (F. Albany Major, Hon. Sec.). To Dollard Printing House, Dublin, for *Gaelic Journal*. 1300 copies. To University Press, Oxford, for Kildare Arch. Soc. 150 copies (Sir Arthur Vickers, Ulster. 22 Ovington Gardens, S. W.) To Messrs. Guy & Co. Ltd., 70 Patrick St, Cork, for Cork Arch. Soc. 450 copies. To Messrs. Marcus Ward & Co. Ltd., Belfast for Ulster Journal of Arch., 1000 copies. (Francis Joseph Bigger Ed., Ardrie, Belfast). To Welsh Cymmrodorian Society. 500 copies. To Waterford Literary Society. 200 copies. To National Literary Society, Dublin. 150. To Gill & Son Publishers, 50, O'Connell St. Upper., Dublin, 200 copies. To J. O'Donoghue Publisher, 3 Bedford Row, Dublin 250-1000 copies.

221 Name of Society above line.
222 Above line.
223 Above line.

LIST OF PAPERS TO WHOM NOTICES SENT.

Mr. Clement Shorten for *Sketch* etc. Mr. C. Graves for *Spectator*. Mr. O'Brien for *Speaker*. Mr. Fisher for 'Literary View'. Mr. Waill for *Literature*. Mr. McCole for *Athaneum*. E. O'Neill? for *Academy*. Miss McDonnell for *Bookman*. Miss O'Reilly for *Pall Mall*. Also to Mr. Wm. Sharp, Mr. Gwynn, Mr. Hickson, Miss Drew, Miss O'C. Eccles, Miss Keeling, Mr. Yeats, Mr. L. Johnson, Mr. Nutt for *Daily Chronicle*, Mr. MacDonagh, Mr. O'Donoghue, *Weekly Sun* etc. For Irish papers. To Mr. Rolleston and Mr. O'Grady for *Express*, *Irish Times* and *Kilkenny Mod.*, Miss A. Oldham for the *Irish Independent*, *Figaro* etc., Miss Milligan, N. Patrick etc., Ed. *New Ireland Review*. Dublin Daily Papers per Miss Borthwick. *Gaelic Journal* and *Fáinne an Lae*, ditto. The Ed. *Clareman*, Ennis, The Ed. *Munster News*, Limerick. Mr. d'Arbois de Jubainville for *Revue Celtique*.

THE IRISH TEXTS SUBCOMMITTEE MET ON JAN. 28TH, 1898.

Present: Mr. Mescal in the Chair, Mr. O'Keeffe, Miss Borthwick, Miss Hull.

A letter was read from Gill & Sons Dublin proposing to aid the Society by issuing its prospectus provided that their name were added to that of the London publisher in the vols. issued by the Society. Miss Hull was instructed to inform them that the books would not be available for sale under ordinary trade regulations, and therefore their suggestion could not be complied with. Letters were read from Prof. Rhys, Dr Whitley Stokes and others expressing sympathy and a report was made as to the progress of the Society.

Mr. Mescal proposed and Miss Hull seconded a resolution that the Irish Literary Society should be asked to advance the necessary funds for the preliminary expenses incurred in making the Society known, circularizing and postage, up to a sum not exceeding £10-0-0 over and above the grant made by the General Committee for printing the first batch of 7000 circulars. The loan to be repaid out of the funds of the Irish Texts[224] Society.

Abraham Colles.[225]

224 Irish Texts above line.

225 Signature of Chairman.

THE IRISH TEXTS SUBCOMMITTEE MET ON FEB. 9TH, 1898.
Present: Dr A. Colles in the Chair, Mr. Mescal, Mr. Macalister, Miss Borthwick, Miss Hull, Mr. Nutt also attended.

The Minutes of last meeting having been read and signed letters were read from Dr Douglas Hyde, Mr. O'Donoghue[226] and Dr Windisch.

Miss Hull was instructed to write to Mr. Hyde authorising him to engage copyists to prepare texts for his volume at an expense of not more than £6 to be defrayed out of the Editorial Funds of the ITS. She was instructed to tell him that while he was authorised to use his own judgement as regards the orthography of texts the Committee would suggest that a distinction should be drawn between errors in orthography arising from ignorance or carelessness, on the part of the scribes, and peculiarities of spelling characteristic of the period at which the MS. was written, and that alterations should be confined as far as possible to the former class.

Mr. Macalister was instructed to write to Prof. Windisch and enquire whether a proposal would be entertained by him and the publisher of the *Irische Texte* to print his edition of the *Táin Bó Cúailnge* with an English instead of a German translation, and to consider some agreement with the Irish Texts Society by which this volume could be distributed to our members as one of our annual publications. Mr. O'Donoghue's letter was referred for consideration to the future Council. Miss Borthwick then stated that she had been informed by the society[227] that Professor Henebry of Washington had in his possession facsimiles of Manus O'Donnell's Life of Columcille and that he had the intention of editing the work.[228] She had written to him for further information on the subject to lay before the Committee. Mr. Nutt made some suggestions as to the formation of the Irish Texts Society and a general discussion followed on the Subject. It was agreed that rules should be drawn up by the Council when elected and that a preliminary list should be prepared of names of persons who should be proposed for the Council of the Society, these names to be submitted in voting papers to the members of the Society for election.

Goddard H. Orpen[229]

226 This is likely to have been Tadhg O'Donoghue (Torna).

227 By the society is above line.

228 The Committee would have been anxious to discover whether this edition would interfere with its own plans for an edition by T. J. Flannery. As it happened, Flannery was willing to leave the edition to Henebry; see below at p. 117.

229 Signature of Chairman.

THE SUB-COMMITTEE MET ON MARCH 3RD, 1898.

Present: Mr. Orpen in the Chair; Messrs. O'Brien, O'Keeffe, Mescal, Macalister, Miss Borthwick and Miss Hull. Mr. Nutt also attended.

The Minutes having been read and signed, a letter was read from Dr Hyde expressing his concurrence with the instructions of the Committee regarding the editorial work he had in hand.

A telegram was read from Prof. York Powell expressing his approval of the idea of a reference committee in addition to a small executive council.[230]

A letter read from Dr Norman Moore[231] and a statement was made giving his opinion in favour of a body of referees to act with the Council, and to give advice on editorial matters. The names of the referees chosen to decide on any special manuscript or proposal submitted to them by the Council to be private, but their opinions to be recorded. After some general discussion, Mr. O'Brien proposed and Mr. Macalister seconded a proposal to appoint a President, Vice President and Council, and to submit these names and the Rules of the Society to a general meeting to be summoned at an early date. Carried.

Mr. O'Brien proposed and Mr. Mescal seconded that the Marquess of Dufferen should be asked to act as President to the Society.[232] Carried.

A provisional list of Vice Presidents and Council was then drawn up as follows:

For Council: Prof. York Powell, Dr Norman Moore, Mr. Flannery, Mr. O'Keeffe, Mr. Mescal, Mr. Orpen, Mr. Nutt (ex officio).[233]

For Vice-Presidents: Dr Hyde, Dr Joyce, Mr. Comyn, Mr. McNeill, Rev. O'Leary, Rev. Dr MacCarthy, Dr Ingram, Rev. Dr Hogan, Most Rev. Dr O'Donnell, Rev. Maxwell Close, Standish Hayes O'Grady, Dr Whitley Stokes, Prof. Rhys, Dr Kuno Meyer, Mr. Strachan; Prof. Mackinnon, Mr. MacBain; Rev. O'Growney, Prof Henebry; Dr Windisch, d'Arbois De Jubainville, Prof. Gaidoz, Prof. Zimmer, Signor Ascoli.[234]

Seumas Ua Caoim.[235]

---

230 The 'reference committee' came to be known as the Consultative Committee.

231 See previous note.

232 Douglas Hyde was subsequently nominated to this position.

233 Moore subsequently refused to allow his name to go forward. The names of G. A. Greene and Mr. O'Sullivan were later added to the list of nominees.

234 For the final list of Vice-Presidents, see below at p. 121. It is interesting to note that Douglas Hyde was first considered for nomination as Vice-President.

235 Signature of Chairman (J. G. O'Keeffe).

THE SUB COMMITTEE MET ON MARCH 10TH, 1898.

Present: Mr. O'Keeffe in the Chair, Messrs. Mescal, Macalister, Mr. Nutt, Miss Hull, Miss Borthwick.

The Minutes having been read and signed a letter was read from Prof. York Powell suggesting the desirability of having a Consultative as well as an Executive council.

A letter from Prof. Henebry was also read making some suggestions about Manus O'Donnell's Life of Columcille etc. It was proposed by Miss Borthwick seconded by Miss Hull that instead of submitting to the General Meeting of the Texts Society three lists, i. e. President, Vice Presidents, Consultative and Executive Councils, we submit four lists, viz. President, Vice-Presidents, Consultative and Executive Councils. Carried.

The former list was then re-arranged, and divided into two parts, some of the members to be asked to act on the Consultative Council and others as Vice Presidents. A question having been raised as to giving[236] special terms to the bookselling trade, the question was referred to the future decision of the Council, but instructions were given that booksellers should join the Society on the same terms as any other member.

Miss Borthwick was instructed to write to Mr. Flannery and make enquiries as to the progress of his work.

Goddard H. Orpen[237]

THE SUB COMMITTEE MET ON MARCH 16TH, 1898.

Mr. Orpen in the Chair. Present Messrs. O'Keeffe, Mescal and Macalister, Miss Borthwick and Miss Hull. Mr. Graves and Mr. Nutt were also present.

A letter was read from Mr. Flannery expressing his willingness to resign his work as editor of Manus O'Donnell's Life of Columcille in favour of Father Henebry, if the latter could have his edition ready in the required time.[238] Miss Borthwick was instructed to write to the latter and ask whether he would give his work to the ITS; when it would be ready and how long the book would be; also to tell him that a translation would be required.

236 Above line.

237 Signature of Chairman.

238 See p. 115 above.

A letter from Dr Hyde stated that he could find only one MS. of *Giolla an Fhiugha*. Mr. Macalister was asked to communicate to him the existence of another copy and to furnish Dr Hyde with a transcription of it.

A letter from Dr Moore contained his refusal to come on the Consultative Council.

The date of the General Meeting was then fixed for Tuesday afternoon, April 26 at 5.30 p.m. and the form of notice was settled.

Mr. Orpen was asked to draw up a draft of rules to be presented to the Meeting for the consideration of the Committee.

Miss Borthwick was instructed to invite Dr T. J. Sheehan to join the Consultative Council.

Some names were added to the proposed list of Vice-Presidents.
Goddard H. Orpen[239]

THE PROVISIONAL COMMITTEE MET ON MARCH 24TH, 1898. The chair was taken by Mr. Goddard Orpen. Present Mr. Nutt, Mr. O'Keeffe, Mr. Mescal, Mr. Macalister, Miss Hull and Miss Borthwick.

The Minutes having been read and signed, letters were read from Prof. Rhys, Dr Ingram, M. Gaidoz, the O'Conor Don, Mr. Bergin, accepting positions on the Consultative Council or as Vice Presidents respectively. And letters from Dr W. Stokes and Dr Graves, Bishop of Limerick, declining. Miss Hull was directed to communicate again with these gentlemen.

Miss Hull also communicated the contents of a letter received by Dr Hyde from Professor Bernard F.T.C.D. stating that the edition of Manus O'Donnell's Life of Colum Cille on which Father Denis Murphy was engaged at the time of his death had been prepared from a fine MS. in the Franciscan Monastery, Dublin, with which any edition prepared from the Bodleian MS. should be compared.[240] Mr. G. Orpen then presented a draft of Rules to be laid before the General Meeting on April 26th and they were discussed and amended and approved.
Goddard H. Orpen[241]

239 Signature of Chairman. 'GHO translated a French book on Socialism of To-day in England about 1885' is added in pencil, possibly by Maurice O'Connell.

240 For more information on Fr Murphy's proposed edition of Colum Cille's Life, see p. 20 above.

241 Signature of Chairman.

THE PROVISIONAL COMMITTEE MET ON APRIL 7TH, 1898.

Mr. Goddard Orpen in the Chair. Present, Mr. O'Keeffe, Mr. Nutt, Mr. Greene, Miss Borthwick and Miss Hull.

The Minutes having been read and signed a letter was read from Mr. Cochrane[242] offering to send out Circulars to the members of R.S.A.I.

Letters were read from Mr. Anwyl, Prof. Mackinnon, Rev. Maxwell Close, Dr Joyce, Dr Zimmer, accepting positions as V. Presidents or as members of Consultative Council, and from Mr. Strachan declining.

A letter was read from Father Henebry declining to undertake Manus O'Donnell's Life of Columcille for the Society. A suggestion that Prof. Thurneysen's name and that of Dr Holger Pedersen[243], should be added to the list of the Consultative committee was adopted. A letter was also read from Rev. T. O'Reilly O. S. F. giving information regarding Father Denis Murphy's edition of the Life of Columcille and offering to open the Franciscan[244] Library to anyone who needed to make use of the MSS for the purposes of the Society. Miss Borthwick was directed to make further inquiries regarding the condition in which[245] Father Murphy's work was left at the time of his death.

Mr. Nutt communicated that Rev. G. Calder, Tyndrum, had made a careful study of the Tógáil Bruidhne Dhá Derga and was preparing an edition of it, and that he (Mr. Nutt) had sent him some proof sheets of Hennessy's corrected by Hennessy himself before his death.[246] A proposal made at the General Meeting of the ILS was then discussed. It was recommended by the General Meeting for the consideration of the Texts Subcommittee that a Public Meeting should be held to stir up interest in the movement. It was decided that the time for such a meeting had not yet come.

Rule XIV was then read and approved. It runs as follows: 'members wishing to resign must give notice in writing to one of the Hon. Secs. before the end of the year of their intention to do so; otherwise they shall be liable for their subscriptions for the ensuing year'.

242 Robert Cochrane was Hon. General Secretary of the R.S.A.I.

243 Pedersen's name added above line.

244 Above line.

245 'the conditon in which' above line.

246 As far as I am aware, there is no other evidence for either scholar's work on an edition of Togail Bruidne Da Derga.

It was decided to ask Prof. Y. Powell to take the Chair at the General Meeting and the agenda was arranged as follows:

1. Statement from Chairman. 2. Adoption of Rules. 3. Election of Officers. 4. Appointment of members, (i) of Consultative Committee, (ii) of Executive Committee. 5. Appointment of Auditors.

The Secretary was authorized to have a stamp made for the Society.

Alfred Nutt[247]

THE PROVISIONAL COMMITTEE MET ON APRIL 21ST, 1898.

Present, Mr. Nutt in the Chair, Mr. O'Keeffe, Mr. Mescal, Miss Borthwick and Miss Hull.

The minutes having been read and signed, Miss Hull read a letter from Mr. Goddard Orpen stating that Prof. York Powell had consented to take the Chair at the General Meeting on April 26th. Miss Borthwick read a letter from Very Rev. Dr Delaney offering the Society the use of the late Rev. Denis Murphy's manuscripts of the Life of Columcille which he forwarded for their inspection. After some discussion, it was decided to make further inquiries as to the orginal from which the transcript was made, and also to endeavour to ascertain the cost of photographing the entire MS. in the Bodleian Library.

A letter from Rev. Eugene O'Growney was read suggesting to the Society the advisability of producing a handy Irish dictionary and it was decided that the matter should be reserved for future consideration.[248] The arrangements for the General Meeting were then discussed. It was decided to add the names of Mr. G. A. Greene M. A. and of Mr. O'Sullivan to the Executive Council and of Lord Castletown to the List of Vice Presidents.[249] It was also decided to put forward only one name viz. Dr Douglas Hyde, for election as President.

Goddard H. Orpen[250] 5. V. 98

247 Signature of Chairman.

248 This was the letter that led to a decision to prepare an Irish-English dictionary. The announcement of the decision to set up a special Sub-Committee to examine the project, published in the appendix to Volume 1 (p. [14]), also used 'handy' to describe the proposed dictionary.

249 Lord Castletown went on to be the longest surviving member of the original list of Vice-Presidents.

250 Signature of Chairman.

Inaugural General Meeting

The Inaugural General Meeting of the Irish Texts Society was held on Tuesday, April 26th 1898. in the Rooms of the Irish Literary Society. The first Chair was taken by Mr. R. Barry O'Brien. On the proposal of Mr. Orpen seconded by Mr. O'Keeffe,[251] Professor York Powell was moved to the Chair.

The Chairman made a statement referring to the necessity that existed for the establishment of such a Society and the part taken by the Irish Literary Society in bringing it into existence. He stated that since the issue of the Prospectus in January last 369 members had joined the Society and £46. 11. 6 had been received in donations towards the Editorial Fund.

The Rules were then read and adopted. Rule 5 was amended as follows: 'All property of the Society shall be vested in the Executive Council, and shall be disposed of as they shall, *by a 2/3 majority*, direct'. Proposed: Mr. Goddard Orpen; Seconder: Miss O'Conor Eccles.

It was proposed by Mr. Greene, seconded by Mr. Nutt, that Dr Douglas Hyde should be asked to take the post of President of the Society and unanimously carried. Miss Borthwick and Miss Hull were re-appointed Hon. Secs. of the Society and Mr. Macalister Hon. Treas. Mr. McCollum having temporarily taken the Chair the following persons[252] were elected[253] for the Executive Council: Mr. Goddard Orpen – Vice Chairman. Mr. Nutt, Mr. Flannery, Mr. O'Keeffe, Mr. Mescal, Mr. Greene, Mr. O'Sullivan.

The following were elected[254] for Vice Presidents: Most Rev. Dr O'Donnell, Bishop of Raphoe, Rev. Maxwell Close, The O'Conor Don, Lord Castletown, Professor Ingram LL.D., F.T.C.D., Dr Shahan, His Eminence[255] Cardinal Moran and Cardinal Gibbons.

The following persons[256] were elected[257] for Consultative Council: Dr Douglas Hyde, Dr Joyce, Messrs. D. Comyn, MacNeill, Flannery,

251 Miss Hull wrote 'unanimously adopted' after O'Keeffe, but this was crossed out by GHO (Goddard Orpen).
252 Corrected from 'names' by GHO.
253 Corrected from 'proposed' by GHO.
254 Corrected from 'proposed' by GHO.
255 Added by GHO.
256 Corrected from 'names' by GHO.
257 Corrected from 'proposed' by GHO.

Bergin, Professors Rhys, Mackinnon, Anwyl, Henebry, Zimmer. Rev. Fathers O'Growney, Hickey, O'Leary. M. Henri Gaidoz, Dr Holger Pedersen.

The following were also to be invited to serve on this Council: Dr W. Stokes, Dr S. H. O'Grady, Dr K. Meyer, Rev. Prof. Hogan, S. J., Rev. Dr MacCarthy. Dr Windisch, M. d'Arbois de Jubainville, Dr Rudolf Thurneysen.

Mr. Frank McDonagh and Mr. Noonan were elected as auditors.

A vote of thanks to the Chairman was proposed by Mr. G. A. Greene and seconded by Mr. Alfred Nutt and unanimously carried.

Goddard H. Orpen,[258] 5. V. 98
R. Barry O'Brien, April 26th, 1899.[259]

258 Signature of Chairman.

259 O'Brien added his signature at the first Annual General Meeting which he chaired.

Chapter Eight

Miscellaneous Documents

1

Text of Circular (1896/7?) Proposing Establishment of Irish Texts Society[260]

Irish Literary Society
Adelphi Terrace
Strand W. C.

Dear Sir,
Many Irishmen have long thought that something might be done for the formation of an *Irish Texts Society* which should concern itself with the publication of part at least of the mass of unprinted poetry and prose still existing in the Irish language.

Whilst gratefully recognising what other Societies have done in the past in this direction – such as the Irish Archaeological Society, the Celtic and Ossianic Societies – mindful also of the work of the Royal Irish Academy, the Society for the Preservation of the Irish Language, the Gaelic Union and some of our existing antiquarian bodies – and gladly acknowledging the valuable and disinterested labours of many continental scholars, we know that most of the literature published by those societies and by those scholars has been *ancient* or *medieval*, whilst the later Irish-Gaelic literature has been neglected or ignored.

It is to deal especially with the later Irish writings – namely those of the last three or four hundred years – that an *Irish Texts Society* has been projected; and it will be seen, therefore, that so far from usurping

260 MS. 10,881 (E. MacNeill), Folder 18 ('E. Hull/ITS'), National Library of Ireland. The Circular, which is dated '1896/7' in added pencil, consists of two leaves (four pages), c. 14cms x 21 cms. The folder contains 14 printed copies.

the place or function of any other society, the new body would only seek to extend and supplement the labours of existing societies.

Whilst concerning itself primarily with poetry or prose in the Irish language, the Irish Texts Society would not necessarly exclude from its province interesting mss. in other languages, as Latin, French, Spanish or the like, if they were such as would throw light on Irish history or Irish social life.

Amongst modern Irish works yet unpublished may be mentioned Keating's *Forus Feasa ar Éirinn* (of which Haliday published only one fourth), the same author's *Eochair-Sciath an Aifrinn*, MacFirbis's *Book of Genealogies*, the *Iomarbaigh na mBard* (or 'Contention of the Bards'), Owen O'Duffy's *Aoir*, The Book of the O'Byrnes, Keating's poems, the *Caithreim Thoirdhealbhaigh* (or 'Triumphs of Turlough O'Brien'), O'Neachtain's *Eachtra Eadhmuinn Ui Chleirigh*, the *Toruigheacht Cheallachain Chaisil*, numerous Ossianic poems, numerous Fenian stories and legends – all these works being but a small part of what remain still in Ireland, without counting the stores in the British Museum or at Oxford or in the continental libraries, and of course not touching at all upon the more ancient texts.

A provisional committee has been formed to discuss the feasibility of such a society, and to make preliminary enquiries. The members of this committee are: D. Comyn (formerly editor of the *Gaelic Journal*), Dr A. Colles, F. A. Fahy, T. J. Flannery, G. A. Greene M. A., D. Hyde, LL.D, MRIA, P. W. Joyce, LL.D, MRIA, J. Mac Neill B. A. (editor, *Gaelic Journal*), J. G. O'Keeffe, Goddard Orpen B.A., G. Sigerson MD, MRIA.

Dr Douglas Hyde MRIA, President of the *Gaelic League* writes:

> 'I d-taoibh Chomainn le texanna Nuadh – Ghaedhilge do thabhairt amach, ta me lan-tsasta ag cloisteal go bh-fuil run agaibh a leitheid do chur ar bun agus bhearfaidh me gach congnamh daoibh is feidir liom.'

Mr. Standish H. O'Grady LL.D has written:

> 'The notion of publishing Irish texts is the best thing I have heard in connection with our Society. No one that I know thinks of deprecating the labours of scientific foreigners, but what is needed now is to invest the whole subject of Irish linguistics with some ordiinary human interest, for we cannot all be German Sanskritists.'

Dr Norman Moore writes:

> 'I suppose that only texts in the Irish language (with translations) will be published, and there are so many of these that the Society might be

fully occupied for many years. I think it would be a pity to limit the period from which the texts are to be selected. Careful editions of any texts would be useful and interesting. If a Society is formed for the publication of texts in Irish, I shall be happy to subscribe.'

Professor York Powell of Oxford writes:

'The editing – beyond securing best texts, exactness of transcript, and adding a very brief preface – would be confined to a very few necessary notes and an English translation … you would have subscribers in Germany and France, as well as in Ireland, Great Britain and the United States of America. Hoping something good for Irish literature and the true knowledge of the old tongue and the old poetry may come out of this, I remain faithfully, etc.'

Mr. John Mac Neill B. A. (editor of the *Gaelic Journal*), writes:

'Ni leir dom aon dioghbhail do bhainfeadh le h-Irisleabhar na Gaedhilge na le Connradh na Gaedhilge de dheascaibh na h-oibre sin. Is amhlaidh mheasaim-se go gcuideochadh an da obair le cheile … Leanaidh den obair seo agus bheurfaidh an t-Irisleabhar gach cabhair daoibh da bh-fuil in acfuinn do.'

It is intended, if the Society be formed, that it shall publish once a year a volume in Irish and its translation in English, either separately or in one book, and each subscriber would be entitled to receive such volumes as they appeared. The editors would be chosen from well-known and competent members of the Irish Texts Society.

An annual subscription of *half a guinea* has been suggested as sufficient to enable such a Society to begin its labours, provided that a fair number of subscribers can be obtained.

The Provisional Committee will be happy to hear if you approve of the proposal for an *Irish Texts Society*, and will be glad to know how far they may rely on your co-operation and support.

Signed,
R. Barry O'Brien C. E., Chairman of the Committee of the Irish Lit. Soc.;
A. P. Graves, Hon. Sec. ;
T. J. Flannery, Sec. Provisional Committee, Irish Texts Society.

P. S. All communications to be addressed to T. J. Flannery (Sec. Provisional Committee), Irish Literary Society, Adelphi Terrace, Strand, W. C.

2

TEXTS OF TWO LETTERS PUBLISHED IN *ATHENAEUM* (19/2/1898) RELATING TO SECOND CIRCULAR ISSUED IN CONNECTION WITH ESTABLISHMENT OF IRISH TEXTS SOCIETY.[261]

Erpingham,
Bedford Park.
Feb. 15, 1898.

With reference to the remarks of your correspondant in last week's *Athenaeum* regarding the Prospectus of the ITS will you allow me to explain that, with the exception of the three texts (as to which no objection is raised) to be edited by Dr Douglas Hyde, Mr. Flannery and Mr. David Comyn respectively, the list of proposed volumes is a purely tentative one? It was, indeed, compiled out of lists furnished by leading Irish scholars, preference in selection being given to texts suggested on more than one such list. It is, however, entirely open to revision, and the committee will always be glad to receive suggestions as to suitable texts, as well as offers of assistance from competent Irish scholars. It was, perhaps, presumptious of us to put so difficult a text as the 'Tain Bo Cuailgne' on our list and we shall certainly be glad if Professor Windisch, by bringing it out, either independently or in concert with us, will relieve us of the difficult task of finding an equally competent editor.

I may add that we have already received a very encouraging response to our circular, showing that the effort to establish an Irish Texts Society is welcomed by many. Intending subscribers should communicate with Mr. R. A. S. Macalister, Honorary Treasurer, Irish Literary Society, Strand WC or Mr. Alfred Nutt, 270, Strand.

Goddard H. Orpen, Chairman, Provisional Committee, ITS

In reference to the note in your last issue, may I inform your contributer that the Prospectus was not only sent to all Irish scholars on the Provisional Committee, including Dr Douglas Hyde, but was also submitted privately to other Irish scholars who have not joined the committee as, for instance, to Dr Norman Moore and to Mr. Standish O'Grady.

---

261 Both of these letters (as published in *Athenaeum*) are in Ms. 25,062 (Hyde), p. 81, National Library of Ireland.

Your contributer takes exception to the inclusion of the 'Knight of the Lion', the Irish version of the well-known Arthurian romance the 'Chevalier du Lion' of Crestian de Troies (sic), the 'Lady of the Fountain' of the Mabinogion. As it was at my suggestion that this and the other Irish Arthurian romances e. g. the earliest known version of the 'Amadan Mor', the metrical version of the 'Mantel Maltaille', etc. were included in the Society's programme, I should like to say that this issue is, to my knowledge, looked forward to with much interest by several continental students of the Arthurian cycle. Texts of this kind have great value for students of romantic literature.

Your contributer seems to take exception to the fact that two Irishwomen are acting as Honorary Secretaries to the proposed society. I venture to think that the zealous and enthusiastic co-operation of Irishwomen with Irishmen in the preservation of the national literature is one of the most encouraging features in the movement which has led to the formation of the Irish Texts Society.

Alfred Nutt.

3

Letter from Eleanor Hull to Eoin Mac Neill, Dated 29/1/1901[262]

Dear Mr. McNeill,
Our Dictionary (Irish-English) is now so well advanced that we have been getting estimates for its printing from our publisher. Mr. Nutt is proposing to us very favourable terms for publication in which the Society will share considerably in any profits the book may hereafter bring in.

We propose to issue an edition either of 5,000 copies or to print 3,000 and then stereotype and should rely a good deal on the aid of our own Society and of the Gaelic League in making known and distributing the book.

262 Ms. 10,881 (Folder 18), E. Mac Neill from E. Hull (ITS), National Library of Ireland.

A great quantity of words are now collected in slip form and these are now being gone through by several workers with Coney's Dictionary on the value of which Mr. Comyn laid great stress and which in fact the workers find to supply many necessary words. One of our members then went through the letter A with O'Reilly but he found so very few words left to be added (of words falling within our scope) that he has come to the conclusion that it will be sufficient if O'Reilly is run through when the first galley proof comes in. There were only some half dozen words in the whole letter A to be added, and those not essential. We should get on quickly if we could get a loan of a few more copies of Coney's Dictionary. We find it very difficult to get copies, and our work has been hindered by want of subdivision. Do you know of anyone who would be so good as to loan a copy for a short time? We would be very careful of any copies lent, and return them safely. We have three but we could use six or seven easily and it would push on the work much faster. I am most anxious to have a good portion through the press this summer and autumn and to get it out, if possible, early in next year. I do not think any other work presses so much as the Dictionary.

Now I come to the main point. Mr. D. Comyn and Fr O'Leary have, as you are aware, kindly consented to act as General Editors, but both are very busy men, and Mr. Comyn is at the moment engaged on his book for us. We are anxious not to [do?] much to distract his attention from this book by throwing upon him heavy work in connection with the Dictionary, and Fr O'Leary, too, has his hands more than full. We feel it necessary, under the circumstances, to appoint a very competent sub-editor to go through the entire series of slips and see the work through the press. It would be left much to his discretion how much help he would obtain from the General Editors either by sending each of them the whole of the letter slips for revisal and suggestion or by merely consulting them at special points. I may say that Fr O'Leary is so fully in possession of our views that I do not contemplate any difficulty arising in this matter from his special views about spelling, and Mr. Comyn, after correspondence with him, has come to the same conclusion. The advice of both editors will be exceedingly valuable on special points, but it will be necessary for the sub-editor to make himself responsible for the main work of supervision. The committee feel that no one could so well undertake the work as yourself if you could see your way to giving the necessary time during the coming months, and they ask me to lay before you the great importance of having the work properly done and made as complete and perfect as possible. We are all aware that your time is very full but we feel so strongly that no one would give the same confidence both to ourselves and the public that we beg you earnestly to consider whether it would be at all possible for you to lay aside any other work for a time and see this Dictionary through.

I think you would find the work well done so far, but there will need to be compression, not only in the omission of unnecessary Irish words but also of *superfluous* English meanings such as ‘nearness, proximity’, ‘keen-edged, close-edged’, in which the second word has no perceptible difference of meaning and might be cut out; genders, in some cases, inflections have, in great part, to be added, some spellings to be corrected, etc. No doubt also, the editors may wish to add words. Mr. O’Sullivan is starting up a grammatical preface with paradigms which will have to be revised (it will be ready in March), and Mr. Hyde suggests the addition of a list of the few words that are quite irregularly pronounced such as *dearbhrathair, mearbhal, colbha*, etc. This, perhaps, could be done here, if supervised by the editors. This would be a very useful list and would probably only occupy a couple of pages. This Dictionary is to consist (as near as possible) of 640 pp. crown 8vo double columns, and to be printed in Dublin. We have not yet finally decided on the printers nor the price, but we think 5/- to the public and 4/- to the members of our own Society will be the very lowest figure at which it can be made to pay its way after careful calculation. It will not be *more* than this; it will be less if we can possibly meet expenses at a lower figure.

As regards the remuneration of the sub-editor, Mr. Nutt offers the sum of £50 for this purpose and we should like to have your views on the subject. It is not much, but we cannot, as a society, risk much. At the same time, if you felt the sum insufficient, we would do all we could to meet your views in some way or other in order to secure the benefit of your assistance. I do hope you may see your way to helping us; it will need someone who is not only a good Irish scholar, but who is businesslike, scholarly and thorough, and who can give a definite number of hours in each week while the thing is going through the press. I do want to issue a really useful and scholarly book, which can afterwards be enlarged and expanded. The men here have worked hard and well and I think it is wonderful how much they have accomplished merely in leisure moments.

Letter A could be placed in your hands *now, at once*, and meanwhile B etc. would be going on and next, letter by letter, in slips. A copyist should also be found immediately to whom you can hand each letter when finished, to copy for press, and when A-E (or so) were ready, printing could begin. All could go on together. We should like to know if you can find a copyist, and if paid, what his terms would be. There is probably a fixed charge for such work. I may say that the slips are very clearly written and would not be difficult to copy; they are also quite in alphabetical order and would be sent so to you.

I think it would be better not to mention this letter to Mr. Comyn or Fr O'Leary as I have not yet informed them of our decision to take this step, but if I have a favourable reply from you, as I earnestly hope we may (sic), I will write to them at once and explain. I hope you would not find it difficult to consult with either of them. If you cannot help us, who can we ask? I had thought of Mr. Osborn Bergin and Mr. O'Shea, but the former, I believe, cannot give time to Dictionary work at present. Can you suggest anyone? I hope, however, that you may see your way to do it yourself.

We should be glad of a reply as soon as possible, and perhaps, if it *is* in the negative, you would return this letter as I think I have stated all the necessary points and it would help me in case the same thing has to be written over again.

As regards your work on the Duanaire Finn; if necessary we could publish the two parts of Keating next year which Mr. D. Comyn can have ready for us. We have not quite decided whether it would be advisable to issue in 1902. This could be discussed later when this [?] matter is decided.

Yours etc, E. Hull.

Bibliography

Alford, N. (1994, London) *The Rhymers' Club: Poets of the Tragic Generation.*

Breathnach, D. & Ní Mhurchú, M. (1986-97, Dublin) *1882-1982: Beathaisnéis*, 5 vols.

Carey, J. (1998, Dublin) *King of Mysteries: Early Irish Religious Writings.*

Casey, D. J. & Rhodes, R. E. (1977, Connecticut) eds, *Views of the Irish Peasantry, 1800-1900.*

Comyn, D. (1898, Dublin) ed., *Díonbhrollach Fórais Feasa ar Éirinn.*

Comparetti, D. (1885; new edn 1997, Princeton) *Vergil in the Middle Ages.*

Elton, O. (1906, Oxford) *Frederick York Powell, vol. I: Memoirs and Letters.*

Flannery, T. (1896, London) ed., *Oisín in the Land of Youth.*

— (1896, London) *For the Tongue of the Gael.*

Fleetwood, J. F. (1951, Dublin) *History of Medicine in Ireland.*

Flower, R. (1926, London) *Catalogue of Irish Manuscripts in the British Museum* 2.

Foster, R. (1997, Oxford) *W. B. Yeats: A Life.*

Greene, G. A. (1880, London) ed., *The Civil Wars in Peru.*

— (1882, London) ed., *The Life of Nelson.*

— (1892, Berlin) trans., Josef Bühlmann, *The Architecture of Classical Antiquity and of the Renaissance.*

— (1893, London) trans., *Italian Lyricists of Today: The Poems of Giosue Carducci.*

— (1912, London) *Songs of the Open Air.*

Greene, G. A., Hillier, A. C. & Dowson, E. (1895, London) trans., Richard Muther, *The History of Modern Painting.*

Hyde, D. (1895, London) *The Story of Early Gaelic Literature.*

Jackson, K. (1990, Dublin) ed., *Aislinge Meic Conglinne.*

MacAirt, S. (1944, Dublin) ed., *Leabhar Branach:The Book of the O'Byrnes.*

Macalister, R. A. S. & MacNeill, E. (1916, Dublin) *Leabhar Gabhála. The Book of Conquests of Ireland. The Recension of Mícheál Ó Cléirigh.*

MacNeill, E. (1919, Dublin) *Phases of Irish History.*

Meyer, K. (1905, Oxford) ed., *Cáin Adamnáin.*

Moore, N. (1882, Cambridge) trans., Ernst Windisch, *A Concise Irish Grammar.*

Nagy, J. F. (1985, Berkeley, Los Angeles, London) *The Wisdom of the Outlaw: the Boyhood Deeds of Finn in Gaelic Narrative Tradition.*
— (1997, Ithaca & London) *Conversing with Ancients and Angels: Literary Myths of Medieval Ireland.*
Ó Buachalla, B. (1987, London) *Foras Feasa ar Éirinn History of Ireland: Foreword to 1987 Reprint.*
— (1996, Dublin) *Aisling Ghéar: na Stíobhartaigh agus an tAos Léinn.*
Ó Conluain, P. & Ó Céileachair, D. (1958, Dublin) *An Duinníneach.*
Ó Dónaill, N. (1977, Dublin) ed., *Foclóir Gaeilge-Béarla.*
Ó Donnchadha, T. (1931, Dublin) ed., *Leabhar Cloinne Aodha Buidhe.*
Ó Duilearga, S. (1956, Dublin) ed., *Seanchas ón Oileán Tiar: Stories told to Robin Flower by Tomás Ó Criomthainn.*
Ó Laoghaire, An t-Ath. Peadar (1904; new edn 1987, Dublin) *Séadna.*
Ó Liatháin, D. (No date, Dublin) *Tomas Ó Flannghaile, Scoláire agus File.*
Ó Lúing, S. (1991, Dublin) *Kuno Meyer 1858-1919.*
Ó Macháin, P. (1990, Dublin) ed., *Catalogue of Irish Manuscripts in the National Library of Ireland* 11.
Ó Raghallaigh, T. (1930, Galway) ed., *Duanta Eoghain Ruaidh Mhic An Bhaird.*
O'Duffy, R. J. (1883, Dublin) ed., *Oidhe Chloinne Lir.*
— (1888, Dublin) ed., *Oidhe Chloinne Tuireann.*
O'Grady, S. H. (1892, London) ed., *Silva Gadelica*, 2 vols.
O'Rahilly, C. (1949, Dublin) ed., *Eachtra Uilliam.*
Olden, T. (1888, Dublin) *The Holy Scriptures in Ireland one Thousand Years Ago.*
Pearse, P. (1918, Dublin) *Collected Works of Padraic H. Pearse: Songs of the Irish Rebels and Specimens from an Irish Anthology.*
Plummer, C. (1925, Brussels) *Miscellanea Hagiographica Hibernica.*
Reid, B. L. (1968, New York) *The Man from New York: John Quinn and his Friends.*
Rhymers' Club (1892, London) ed., *The Book of the Rhymers' Club.*
— (1894, London) ed., *The Second Book of the Rhymers' Club.*
Russell, T. O'Neill (1901, Dublin) ed., *An Bhoramha Laighean.*
Ryan, M. (1946, Dublin) *Fenian Memories.*
Ryan, W. P. (1894, London) *The Irish Literary Revival.*
Scott, A. B. & Martin, F. X. (1978, Dublin) eds, Giraldus Cambrensis's *Expugnatio Hibernica.*
Sloan, J. (1995, Oxford) ed., *Selected Poems and Prose of John Davidson.*
Stokes, W. (1905, London) ed., *Félire Oengusso.*
Williams, N. J. A. (1981, Dublin) ed., *Páirlement Chloinne Tomáis.*
Windisch, E. (1880, Leipzig) ed., *Irische Texte mit Wörterbuch.*

General Index

Kevin Murray

IRISH TEXTS SOCIETY

Cumann na Scríbheann nGaedhilge

1998

OBJECTS • SUBSCRIPTION
OFFICERS AND COUNCIL
LIST OF PUBLICATIONS

IRISH TEXTS SOCIETY,
c/o THE ROYAL BANK OF SCOTLAND PLC,
DRUMMONDS BRANCH, 49 CHARING CROSS,
ADMIRALTY ARCH, LONDON SW1A 2DX

IRISH TEXTS SOCIETY

The Irish Texts Society, founded in 1898, is established to advance public education by promoting the study of Irish literature, and as ancillary thereto to publish texts in the Irish language, accompanied by such introductions, English translations, glossaries and notes as may be deemed desirable.

MEMBERSHIP

Membership is open to individuals and libraries.

The Annual Subscription is payable on the 1st January.

INDIVIDUAL MEMBERSHIP:

*Annual subscription £9 stg., IR£9, US$15.
*Benefits: – Entitled to all new publications at a special price (approximately 50% of retail price).
– Any two back volumes of main series at half price plus postage in any one year.
– Volumes supplied in response to orders.

LIBRARY MEMBERSHIP (two options:)

Option 1: Full Library Membership
(directly or through agents)

*Annual subscription £9 stg., IR£9, US$15.
*Benefits: – Entitled to all new publications at a special price (approximately 50% of retail price).
– Any two back volumes of main series at half price plus postage in any one year.
– Volumes supplied in response to orders.

Option 2: Library Circulation Membership
(directly or through agents)

*No Annual Subscription
*Benefits: – All new publications automatically sent directly to library. Payment against invoice.
– Full retail price to apply. Society to bear the cost of postage.
– All existing publications available on request at full retail price. Society to bear the cost of postage. Payment against invoice.

Non-members can obtain the Society's publications by placing an order with their usual bookseller.

In case of difficulty, they should contact the Honorary Secretary of the Society or ÁIS (Book Distribution Centre), 31 Fenian Street, Dublin 2, Ireland.

PRICES OF VOLUMES

(for currencies not quoted please use the sterling equivalent)

Volume 49 (members only)	**£14 stg., IR£14, US $26**
Volumes 19, 20, 21, 24, 26, 27, 29, 29a, 38, 46, 47, 53, 54, 55	**£16 stg., IR£16, US $30**
Volumes 11, 13, 17, 18, 25, 37, 40, 51, 52	**£18 stg., IR£18, US $34**
Volumes 4, 8, 9, 15, 30, 31, 32, 33, 34, 35, 39, 41, 42, 45, 48, 50	**£20 stg., IR£20, US $38**
Volume 1	**£25 stg., IR£25, US $45**
Volumes 6, 10	**£30 stg., IR£30, US $54**
Volumes 12, 22, 23, 36, 56	**£32 stg., IR£32, US $60**
Volumes 2, 3a, 5, 7, 14, 16, 28, 43, 44, 57	**£34 stg., IR£34, US $64**

OTHER PUBLICATIONS

Dinneen's IRISH-ENGLISH DICTIONARY
£25 stg., IR£25, US $45 (members – £15 stg., IR£15, US $27)

Father Dinneen – His Dictionary and the Gaelic Revival
£2 stg., IR£2, US $5 (incl. postage)

Foras Feasa ar Éirinn: History of Ireland. Foreword to 1987 reprint.
£4 stg., IR£4, US $8 (incl. postage)

A New Introduction to the Bardic Poems of Tadhg Dall Ó hUiginn (1550-1591)
£2 stg., IR£2, US $5 (incl. postage)

SUBSIDIARY PUBLICATION SERIES

Nos. 1, 2, 3, 4, 7, 8	**£5 stg., IR£5, US $9 (incl. postage) (members £4 stg., IR£4, US $7)**
Nos. 5, 9	**£12 stg., IR£12, US $22 (members £10 stg., IR£10, US $18)**
No. 6	**£20 stg., IR£20, US $36 (members £16 stg., IR£16, US $30)**

SPECIALLY BOXED SETS

FORAS FEASA AR ÉIRINN (volumes 4, 8, 9, 15)
£120 stg., IR£120, US $225 (members – £60 stg., IR£60, US $115)

CINNLAE AMHLAOIBH UÍ SHÚILEABHÁIN (volumes 30, 31, 32, 33)
£150 stg., IR£150, US $280 (members – £90 stg., IR£90, US $170)

POSTAGE PER VOLUME

Britain & Ireland: £2 stg., IR£2. Surface Mail USA: $6
All other countries: £3 stg. or equivalent

PAYMENT METHODS

Subscriptions:	The Society has a preference, where possible, for Bankers Orders. Other methods, as listed under volumes, are also acceptable.
Volumes:	Cheques, Bank Drafts, and Credit Cards (Visa, Access, Eurocard, Mastercard) may be used to pay for volumes.
Order Forms:	See pp. 15, 16 below

COMMUNICATION

The official address of the Society is as shown on the front page of this List of Publications.

To expedite correspondence, please use the following:

For orders of books, applications/queries re membership, write to: **M. J. Burns, Hon. Treas. I.T.S., Elsemere, Tibradden Road, Rockbrook, Dublin 16, Ireland.**

All other correspondence, write to: **Seán Hutton, Hon. Sec. I.T.S., 69A Balfour Street, London SE17 1PL, United Kingdom.**

LIST OF IRISH TEXTS SOCIETY'S PUBLICATIONS

	** Out of Print*	*Issued*

1 **GIOLLA AN FHIUGHA**
The Lad of the Ferule
Eachtra Cloinne Rígh na h-Ioruaidhe
Adventures of the Children of the King of Norway
DOUGLAS HYDE, ed.
xx + 208 pp. ISBN 1 870 16601 9 1899

2 **FLED BRICREND**
The Feast of Bricriu: an Early Gaelic Saga transcribed from older mss. into the Book of the Dun Cow... with conclusion from Gaelic ms. xl. Edinburgh Advocates Library.
GEORGE HENDERSON, ed.
lxviii + 218 pp. ISBN 1 870 16602 7 1899

3 **DÁNTA AODHAGÁIN UÍ RATHAILLE**
The Poems of Egan O'Rahilly
PATRICK S. DINNEEN, TADHG O'DONOGHUE, ed.
lxii + 360 PP. ISBN 1 870 16603 5 1911

4 **FORAS FEASA AR ÉIRINN**
The History of Ireland by Geoffrey Keating, D.D.
Vol. 1 (See Vols. 8, 9, 15).
DAVID COMYN, ed.
This volume contains Breandán Ó Buachalla's new introduction (1987)
xviii + 238 pp. ISBN 1 870 16604 3 1901

5 **CAITHRÉIM CONGHAIL CLÁIRINGHNIGH**
Martial Career of Conghal Cláiringhneach
PATRICK M. MACSWEENEY, ed.
lxviii + 234 pp. ISBN 1 870 16605 1 1904

6 **IMTHEACHTA AENIASA**
The Irish Aeneid being a Translation, made before A.D. 1400, of the xii Books of Vergil's Aeneid into Gaelic.
GEORGE CALDER, ed.
This volume contains Erich Poppe's new introduction (1995)
xx + 238 pp. ISBN 1 870 16606 X 1907

7 **DUANAIRE FINN**
The Book of the Lays of Fionn
Irish Text with Translation. Part I (See Vols. 28, 43)
EOIN MACNEILL, ed.
lxviii + 208 pp. ISBN 1 870 16607 8 1908

See page 4 for prices of Volumes

8 **FORAS FEASA AR ÉIRINN**
The History of Ireland by Geoffrey Keating, D.D.
Vol. II (See Vols. 4, 9, 15)
PATRICK S. DINNEEN, ed.
xxxvi + 426 pp. ISBN 1 870 16608 6 1908

9 **FORAS FEASA AR ÉIRINN**
The History of Ireland by Geoffrey Keating, D.D.
Vol. III (See Vols. 4, 8, 15)
PATRICK S. DINNEEN, ed.
viii + 388 pp. ISBN 1 870 16609 4 1908

10 **TWO IRISH ARTHURIAN ROMANCES**
Eachtra an Mhadra Mhaoil, Eachtra Mhacaoimh-an-Iolair
The Story of The Crop Eared Dog, the Story of Eagle Boy
R. A. STEWART MACALISTER, ed.
This volume contains a new introduction by Joseph Falaky Nagy (1997)
x + 208 pp. ISBN 1 870 16610 8 1908

11 **DUANAIRE DHÁIBHIDH UÍ BHRUADAIR**
The Poems of David Ó Bruadair
Part I, containing poems down to the year 1666. (See Vols. 13, 18)
JOHN C. MACERLEAN, ed.
lii + 208 pp. ISBN 1 870 16611 6 1910

12 **BUILE SUIBHNE**
(The Frenzy of Suibhne)
Being the Adventures of Suibhne Geilt: A Middle Irish Romance
J. G. O'KEEFFE, ed.
This volume contains a new introduction by Joseph Falaky Nagy (1996)
xxxviii + 198 pp. ISBN 1 870 16612 4 1913

13 **DUANAIRE DHÁIBHIDH UÍ BHRUADAIR**
The Poems of David Ó Bruadair
Part II, containing poems from the years 1667 till 1682. (See Vols. 11, 18)
JOHN C. MACERLEAN, ed.
xl + 288 pp. ISBN 1 870 16613 2 1913

14 **AN IRISH ASTRONOMICAL TRACT**
Based in part on a Medieval Latin version of a work by Messahalah
MAURA POWER, ed.
xviii + 176 pp. ISBN 1 870 16614 0 1914

See page 4 for prices of Volumes

15 **FORAS FEASA AR ÉIRINN**
The History of Ireland by Geoffrey Keating, D.D.
Part IV (see Vols. 4, 8, 9) containing the Genealogies, Synchronisms with an Index, which includes the elucidation of place names and annotations to the text of Vols. I, II and III.
PATRICK S. DINNEEN, ed.
484 pp. ISBN 1 870 16615 9 1914

16 **LIFE OF ST. DECLAN OF ARDMORE AND LIFE OF ST. MOCHUDA OF LISMORE**
P. POWER, ed.
xxxii + 202 pp. ISBN 1 870 16616 7 1914

17 **AMHRÁIN CHEARBHALLÁIN**
The Poems of Carolan, together with other N. Connacht and S. Ulster Lyrics
TOMÁS Ó MÁILLE, ed.
xviii + 424 pp. ISBN 1 870 16617 5 1916

18 **DUANAIRE DHÁIBHIDH UÍ BHRUADAIR**
The Poems of David Ó Bruadair
Part III, containing poems from the year 1682 till the poet's death in 1698. (See Vols. 11, 13)
JOHN C. MACERLEAN, ed.
xvi + 276 pp. ISBN 1 870 16618 3 1917

19 **GABHÁLTAIS SHEARLUIS MHÓIR**
The Conquests of Charlemagne
DOUGLAS HYDE, ed.
xvi + 128 pp. + iv ISBN 1 870 16619 1 1919

20 **IOMARBHÁGH NA BHFILEADH**
The Contention of the Bards, Part I
L. MCKENNA, ed.
This volume contains a new introduction by Joep Leerssen.
xxx + 177 pp. ISBN 1 870 16620 5 1920

21 **IOMARBHÁGH NA BHFILEADH**
The Contention of the Bards Part II
L. MCKENNA, ed.
178-284 pp. ISBN 1 870 16621 3 1920

22 **A BHFUIL AGUINN DÁR CHUM TADHG DALL Ó HUIGINN**
The Bardic Poems of Tadhg Dall Ó hÚiginn (1550-1591)
Vol. I, Text.
ELEANOR KNOTT, ed.
This volume contains a new introduction by P. A. Breatnach (1997).
cviii + 280 pp. ISBN 1 870 16622 1 1922

See page 4 for prices of Volumes

23 **A BHFUIL AGUINN DÁR CHUM TADHG DALL Ó HUIGINN**
The Bardic Poems of Tadhg Dall Ó hÚiginn (1550-1591)
Vol. II, Translation.
ELEANOR KNOTT, ed.
viii + 360 pp. ISBN 1 870 16623 X 1926

24 **TÓRUIGHEACHT GRUAIDHE GRIANSHOLUS**
The Pursuit of Gruaidh Grian-Sholus
CECILE O'RAHILLY, ed.
xxx + 158 pp. ISBN 1 870 16624 8 1924

25 **ROSA ANGLICA SEU ROSA MEDICINAE JOHANNIS ANGLICI**
An Early Modern Irish Translation of Part of John of Gaddesden's Text-Book of Medieval Medicine
WINIFRED P. WULFF, ed.
lviii + 436 pp. ISBN 1 870 16625 6 1929

26 **CAITHRÉIM THOIRDHEALBHAIGH**
The Triumphs of Turlough
Vol. I, Text
STANDISH HAYES O'GRADY, ED.
xvi + 238 pp. ISBN 1 870 16626 4 1929

27 **CAITHRÉIM THOIRDHEALBHAIGH**
The Triumphs of Turlough
Vol. II, Translation
STANDISH HAYES O'GRADY, ed.
vi + 252 pp. ISBN 1 870 16627 2 1929

28 **DUANAIRE FINN**
The Book of the Lays of Fionn.
Irish Text with Translation. Part II. (See Vols. 7, 43).
GERARD MURPHY, ed.
xx + 410 pp. ISBN 1 870 16628 0 1933

29 **INSTRUCTIO PIE VIVENDI ET SUPERNA MEDITANDI**
Instruction in Holy Life and Heavenly Thought.
Vol. I, Latin and Irish versions with Glossary of Irish Words.
JOHN MACKECHNIE, ed.
xiv + 230 +8 ISBN 1 870 16629 9 1934

29a **INSTRUCTIO PIE VIVENDI ET SUPERNA MEDITANDI**
Instruction in Holy Life and Heavenly Thought.
Vol. II, English Translation of the Irish version.
JOHN MACKECHNIE, ed.
xvi + 112 pp. ISBN 1 870 16699 X 1946

See page 4 for prices of Volumes

30 **CINNLAE AMHLAOIBH UÍ SHÚILEABHÁIN**
The Diary of Humphrey O'Sullivan.
Part I, containing the Diary from 1st January, 1827 to the end of August, 1828.
MICHAEL MCGRATH, ed.
lii + 336 pp. ISBN 1 870 16630 2 1936

31 **CINNLAE AMHLAOIBH UÍ SHÚILEABHÁIN**
The Diary of Humphrey O'Sullivan.
Part II, containing the Diary from 1st September, 1828 to the end of December, 1830.
MICHAEL MCGRATH, ed.
vi + 374 pp. ISBN 1 870 16631 0 1936

32 **CINNLAE AMHLAOIBH UÍ SHÚILEABHÁIN**
The Diary of Humphrey O'Sullivan.
Part III, containing the Diary from 1st January, 1831 to the end of December, 1833.
MICHAEL MCGRATH, ed.
xvi + 272 pp. ISBN 1 870 16632 9 1937

33 **CINNLAE AMHLAOIBH UÍ SHÚILEABHÁIN**
The Diary of Humphrey O'Sullivan.
Part IV, containing the Diary for 1834-1835 (to July), Poems, Miscellaneous Sketches, Vocabularies, etc.
MICHAEL MCGRATH, ed.
xlvi + 392 pp. ISBN 1 870 16633 7 1937

34 **LEBOR GABÁLA ÉRENN**
The Book of the Taking of Ireland, Part I.
R. A. S. MACALISTER, ed.
This volume contains John Carey's new introduction (1993)
xxxiv + 270 pp. ISBN 1 870 16634 5 1938

35 **LEBOR GABÁLA ÉRENN**
The Book of the Taking of Ireland, Part II.
R. A. S. MACALISTER, ed.
viii + 274 pp. ISBN 1 870 16635 3 1939

36 **SGÉALTA THOMÁIS UÍ CHATHASAIGH**
Mayo Stories told by Thomas Casey
Hull Memorial Volume
DOUGLAS HYDE, ed.
xxiv + 388 pp. ISBN 1 870 16636 1 1939

37 **AITHDIOGHLUIM DÁNA**
A Miscellany of Irish Bardic Poetry, Historical and Religious, including the Historical Poems of the Duanaire in the Yellow Book of Lecan.
Vol. I, Introduction and Text
LAMBERT MCKENNA, ed.
xxxvi + 362 pp. ISBN 1 870 16637 X 1939

See page 4 for prices of Volumes

38 **STAIR ERCUIL OCUS A BÁS**
The Life and Death of Hercules
GORDON QUIN, ed.
xl + 264 pp. ISBN 1 870 16638 8 1939

39 **LEBOR GABÁLA ÉRENN**
The Book of the Taking of Ireland, Part III.
R. A. S. MACALISTER, ed.
vi + 206 pp. ISBN 1 870 16639 6 1940

40 **AITHDIOGHLUIM DÁNA**
A Miscellany of Irish Bardic Poetry, Historical and Religious, including the Historical Poems of the Duanaire in the Yellow Book of Lecan.
Vol. II, Translation, Notes, Vocabulary.
LAMBERT MCKENNA, ed.
vi + 364 pp. ISBN 1 870 16640 X 1940

41 **LEBOR GABÁLA ÉRENN**
The Book of the Taking of Ireland, Part IV.
R. A. S. MACALISTER, ED.
vi + 342 pp. ISBN 1 870 16641 8 1941

42 **BEATHA AODHA RUAIDH UÍ DHOMHNAILL**
The Life of Aodh Ruadh O Domhnaill
Part I, Text and Translation
PAUL WALSH, ed.
xii + 350 pp. ISBN 1 870 16642 6 1948

43 **DUANAIRE FINN**
Part III (see Vols. 7, 28), Introduction, Notes, Appendices, Indexes and Glossary.
GERARD MURPHY, ANNE O'SULLIVAN, IDRIS L. FOSTER, BRENDAN JENNINGS, ed.
cxxii + 452 pp. ISBN 1 870 16643 4 1953

44 **LEBOR GABÁLA ÉRENN**
The Book of the Taking of Ireland, Part V.
R. A. S. MACALISTER, ed.
viii + 580 pp. ISBN 1 870 16644 2 1956

45 **BEATHA AODHA RUAIDH UÍ DHOMHNAILL**
The Life of Aodh Ruadh O Domhnaill
Part II, Introduction, Glossary, etc.
PAUL WALSH, COLM O LOCHLAINN, ed.
viii + 468 pp. ISBN 1 870 16645 0 1957

See page 4 for prices of Volumes

46 **LEBOR NA CERT**

The Book of Rights

MYLES DILLON, ed.

xxvi + 200 pp. ISBN 1 870 16646 9 1962

47 **THE POEMS OF BLATHMAC SON OF CÚ BRETTAN TOGETHER WITH THE IRISH GOSPEL OF THOMAS AND A POEM ON THE VIRGIN MARY**

JAMES CARNEY, ed.

xl + 170 pp. ISBN 1 870 16647 7 1964

48 **TÓRUIGHEACHT DHIARMADA AGUS GHRÁINNE**

The Pursuit of Diarmaid and Gráinne

NESSA NÍ SHÉAGHDHA, ed.

xxxii + 148 pp. ISBN 1 870 16648 5 1967

49 **TÁIN BÓ CÚALNGE FROM THE BOOK OF LEINSTER**

CECILE O'RAHILLY, ed.

Special arrangement by courtesy of the Dublin Institute for Advanced Studies, limited to members only.

lvi + 356 pp. ISBN 1 870 16649 3 1969

50 **CATH MAIGE MUCRAMA**

The Battle of Mag Mucrama

MÁIRÍN O DALY, ed.

viii + 158 pp. ISBN 1 870 16650 7 1975

51 **THE POEMS OF GIOLLA BRIGHDE MAC CONMIDHE**

NICHOLAS WILLIAMS, ed.

iv + 386 pp. ISBN 1 870 16651 5 1980

52 **CATH MAIGE TUIRED**

The Second Battle of Mag Tuired

ELIZABETH A. GRAY, ed.

vi + 142 pp. ISBN 1 870 16652 3 1982

53 **POEMS ON MARCHER LORDS**

From a Sixteenth-Century Tipperary Manuscript.

ANNE O'SULLIVAN, PÁDRAIG Ó RIAIN, ed.

xxviii + 146 pp. ISBN 1 870 16653 1 1987

54 **BETHA ADAMNÁIN**

The Irish Life of Adamnán

MÁIRE HERBERT, PÁDRAIG Ó RIAIN, ed.

xii + 110 pp. ISBN 1 870 16654 X 1988

See page 4 for prices of Volumes

55 **STAIR NICOMÉID**
The Irish Gospel of Nicodemus
IAN HUGHES, ed.
xlvi + 138 pp. ISBN 1 870 16655 8 1991

56 **OIDHEADH CHLOINNE hUISNEACH**
The Violent Death of the Children of Uisneach
CAOIMHÍN MAC GIOLLA LÉITH, ed.
220 pp. ISBN 1 870 16656 6 1992

57 **BEATHA BHARRA**
Saint Finbarr of Cork: The Complete Life
PÁDRAIG Ó RIAIN, ed.
xviii + 322 pp. ISBN 1 870 16657 4 1994

SUBSIDIARY PUBLICATION SERIES

In the case of all publications in this series, the intention is to introduce the relevant text to a non-specialist readership in a way calculated to make the content more accessible and also to convey an application of its status and significance within its particular genre, literary, historical, etc. Additionally, in the case of texts already published by the Society, the intention of the Subsidiary Series (published in conjunction with the main series of texts) is to take the opportunity of a reprint to update the original introduction by noting the main developments in the field since the original publication. In such circumstances, these publications are included as additional introductory material. They are also published independently as moderately priced booklets with a view to making them available to interested readers who may not necessarily wish to acquire the reprint of the relevant text.

1. John Carey
A New Introduction to Lebor Gabála Érenn, The Book of the Taking of Ireland, Edited and Translated by R. A. Stewart Macalister, D.Litt.
22 pp. 1993. ISBN 1 870166 80 9.

2. Joep Leerssen
The Contention of the Bards (Iomarbhágh na bhFileadh) and its Place in Irish P olitical and Literary History.
72 pp. 1994. ISBN 1 870166 81 7.

See page 4 for prices of Volumes

3. Erich Poppe
A New Introduction to Imtheachta Aeniasa: The Irish Aeneid – the Classical Epic from an Irish Perspective.
40 pp. 1995. ISBN 1 870166 82 5.

4. Joseph Falaky Nagy
A New Introduction to Buile Suibhne (The Frenzy of Suibhne) being The Adventures of Suibhne Geilt: A Middle Irish Romance.
32 pp. 1996. ISBN 1 870166 83 3.

5. Pádraig Ó Riain
The Making of a Saint: Finbarr of Cork 600-1200.
152 pp. 1997. ISBN 1 870166 84 1.

6. Diarmuid Ó Murchadha
The Annals of Tigernach: Index of Names.
ix + 222 pp. 1997. ISBN 1 870166 85 X.

7. Joseph Falaky Nagy
A New Introduction to Two Irish Arthurian Romances.
18 pp. 1998. ISBN 1 870177 86 8.

8. Maire Ní Mhaonaigh
A New Introduction to Giolla na Fhiugha (The Lad of the Ferule) and Eachtra Cloinne Rígh na h-Ioruaidhe (Adventures of the Children of the King of Norway).
32 pp. 1998. ISBN 1 870166 87 6.

9. Pádraig Ó Riain, ed.
Irish Texts Society: The First Hundred Years
142 pp. 1998. ISBN 1 870166 88 4.

See page 4 for prices of Volumes

OTHER PUBLICATIONS

Patrick S. Dinneen, ed.

FOCLÓIR GAEDHILGE AGUS BÉARLA: An Irish-English Dictionary.

1340 pp. 1927. ISBN 1 870 16600 0.

Noel O'Connell

Father Dinneen – His Dictionary and the Gaelic Revival. 8 pp.

Breandán Ó Buachalla

FORAS FEASA AR ÉIRINN: HISTORY OF IRELAND.

Foreword to 1987 Reprint. 8 pp. 1987.

Pádraig A. Breathnach

A NEW INTRODUCTION TO THE BARDIC POEMS OF TADHG DALL Ó hUIGINN (1550-1591). 8 pp.

NEW VOLUMES AND REPRINTS

Volume 56: Caoimhín Mac Giolla Léith, ed., **Oidheadh Chloinne hUisneach: The Violent Death of the Children of Uisneach**

This is the Early Modern Irish version of what is sometimes referred to as 'The Deirdre Story'. It is one of the most popular of the late medieval Gaelic Romances, forming one of a group known as 'The Three Sorrows of Storytelling'. The editor, Dr. Caoimhín Mac Giolla Léith of University College, Dublin, has provided a lengthy introduction exploring the relationship between this text and other versions of the Deirdre story.

Volume 57: Pádraig Ó Riain, ed., **Beatha Bharra: St. Finbarr of Cork, The Complete Life**

'Where Finbarr taught, let Munster learn'. The Society's new volume for 1993, which is edited by Professor Pádraig Ó Riain of University College, Cork, contains the most comprehensive edition ever attempted of an Irish saint's life. In his introduction, Professor Ó Riain, who has written extensively on the subject, traces the origins and development of Finbarr's recorded legend, including the story of his school.

Volume 10: R. A. Stewart Macalister, ed., **Two Irish Arthurian Romances**

The first of the two Arthurian tales, Eachtra an Mhadra Mhaoil 'The Story of the Crop Eared Dog', concerns Sir Gawain and includes accounts of marvellous happenings in Egypt, Greece and other countries. It was composed in Ireland in the fifteenth century. The second tale, Eachtra Mhacaoimh an Iolair 'The Story of Eagle Boy', is an Irish adaptation of a French tale.

See page 4 for prices of Volumes

Cumann na Scríbheann nGaedhilge
IRISH TEXTS SOCIETY

IRISH TEXTS SOCIETY
c/o THE ROYAL BANK OF SCOTLAND PLC,
DRUMMONDS BRANCH, 49 CHARING CROSS,
ADMIRALTY ARCH, LONDON SW1A 2DX

APPLICATION FOR LIBRARY MEMBERSHIP

To: The Honorary Secretary Date: __________

I wish to apply for Full*/Circulation* Membership of the Irish Texts Society
*(*delete as appropriate)*

Name of Library: ____________________
(BLOCK CAPITALS)

Address: ____________________

____

Authorised by: ____________________

Title: ____________________

Date: ____________________

Payment of Full Membership Subscription and Order for Volumes

Volume numbers ____________________

Amount for Volumes £ __________

Postage & Packing £ __________

Subscription £ __________

Total Amount £ __________

If you wish to pay future annual subscriptions by Bankers Order please tick the box and the appropriate form will be sent to you. ☐

(Only complete the following if different from information given above or if you are an existing member).

Name: ____________________

Address: ____________________

____

We enclose herewith Cheque/Bank Draft in the amount of £_____ re the above order.

Please debit our Credit Card. Number: ____________ Expiry Date: __________

Visa ☐ Access ☐ Eurocard ☐ Mastercard ☐

Signature: ____________________

Cumann na Scríbheann nGaedhilge
IRISH TEXTS SOCIETY

IRISH TEXTS SOCIETY
c/o THE ROYAL BANK OF SCOTLAND PLC,
DRUMMONDS BRANCH, 49 CHARING CROSS,
ADMIRALTY ARCH, LONDON SW1A 2DX

APPLICATION FOR INDIVIDUAL MEMBERSHIP

To: The Honorary Secretary Date: __________

I wish to apply for Individual Membership of the Irish Texts Society
*(*delete as appropriate)*

Name: ______________________________
(BLOCK CAPITALS)

Address: ______________________________

____

Occupation: ______________________________

Signature: ______________________________

Payment of Full Membership Subscription and Order for Volumes

Volume numbers ______________________________

Amount for Volumes £ __________

Postage & Packing £ __________

Subscription £ __________

Total Amount £ __________

If you wish to pay future annual subscriptions by Bankers Order please tick the box and the appropriate form will be sent to you. ☐

(Only complete the following if different from information given above or if you are an existing member).

Name: ______________________________

Address: ______________________________

____

I enclose herewith Cheque/Bank Draft in the amount of £_____ re the above order.

Please debit my Credit Card. Number: ____________ Expiry Date: __________

Visa ☐ Access ☐ Eurocard ☐ Mastercard ☐

Signature: ______________________________

PRINTED BY ELO PRESS LTD., DUBLIN 8, IRELAND.